The Archaeology of Forts and Battlefields

The American Experience in Archaeological Perspective

UNIVERSITY PRESS OF FLORIDA

Florida A&M University, Tallahassee
Florida Atlantic University, Boca Raton
Florida Gulf Coast University, Ft. Myers
Florida International University, Miami
Florida State University, Tallahassee
New College of Florida, Sarasota
University of Central Florida, Orlando
University of Florida, Gainesville
University of North Florida, Jacksonville
University of South Florida, Tampa
University of West Florida, Pensacola

The Archaeology of Forts and Battlefields

DAVID R. STARBUCK

Foreword by Michael S. Nassaney

University Press of Florida

Gainesville ▪ Tallahassee ▪ Tampa ▪ Boca Raton

Pensacola ▪ Orlando ▪ Miami ▪ Jacksonville ▪ Ft. Myers ▪ Sarasota

First cloth printing, 2011
First paperback printing, 2012

LIBRARY OF CONGRESS CATALOGING-IN-PUBLICATION DATA
Starbuck, David R.
The archaeology of forts and battlefields / David R. Starbuck ; foreword by Michael S. Nassaney.
p. cm. — (The American experience in archaeological perspective)
Includes bibliographical references and index.
ISBN 978-0-8130-3689-2 (cloth: alk. paper)
ISBN 978-0-8130-4414-9 (pbk.)
　　　1. Battlefields—United States. 2. Excavations (Archaeology)—United States. 3. United States—
History, Military—18th century. 4. United States—History, Military—19th century.
5. Archaeology and history—United States. 6. Fortification—United States—History.
7. United States—Antiquities. I. Title.
E181.S83　2011
973—dc22　2011011285

The University Press of Florida is the scholarly publishing agency for the State University System
of Florida, comprising Florida A&M University, Florida Atlantic University, Florida Gulf Coast
University, Florida International University, Florida State University, New College of Florida, University of Central Florida, University of Florida, University of North Florida, University of South
Florida, and University of West Florida.

University Press of Florida
15 Northwest 15th Street
Gainesville, FL 32611-2079
http://www.upf.com

Contents

Figures

Foreword

Forts and battlefields were essential places in the European exploration and settlement of North America and the means by which Americans struggled to forge a new identity apart from their English forebears. Conflict, defense, and aggression were also central to America's territorial expansion from sea to shining sea. Thus it comes as no surprise that forts and battlefields have long been commemorated by the National Park Service as places that played an important role in creating a national consciousness that served to legitimize the formative actions of our ancestors, who fought and died for their beliefs and principles of sovereignty, freedom, and individualism. The act of commemoration often involved restoration or reconstruction and required evidence for the location of features, the movements of combatants, and soldiers' lifeways.

Although the tactics and strategies employed to possess and defend America changed from the earliest European settlements through the nineteenth century, forts were critical in taking and maintaining control of large reaches of the continent beginning with well known places like James Fort, Fort Michilimackinac, and Fort William Henry, to name just a few. Skirmishes, battles, and military settlements have long attracted the interest of history buffs and professional archaeologists, both of whom recognize "value" in the material remains of warriors such as buckles, buttons, ammunition, and armaments. Because of the popularity of forts and battlefields, their material record has been compromised. Locals frequently robbed abandoned forts of construction materials and settlements that grew up at these strategic locations involved destructive land modifications that negatively impacted the archaeology. Nevertheless, predictable finds at these types of sites include foundations of various buildings, stockade walls, structural debris, privies, earthworks, and numerous artifact classes reflecting domestic, commercial, personal, leisure, and of course military activities.

Not surprisingly, underrepresented populations away from urban centers often left a paucity of written records needed to understand the way in which cultural practices were enacted in geographically marginal and isolated places among artificial communities in interaction with strangers, allies, and enemies. Naturally, this is where archaeology can shine the brightest light.

In *The Archaeology of Forts and Battlefields,* David Starbuck discusses how archaeologists have examined a range of military-related sites including forts, encampments, cantonments, prisons, and battlefields. He notes that, as is often the case, historical archaeologists can use the material remains of conflict to distinguish differences between expected behaviors and the actual activities performed on the ground. Perhaps this is no more apparent than at the Battle of the Little Bighorn, where archaeological investigations have led to a complete retelling of "Custer's Last Stand," forcing us to reconsider long-held assumptions about the man and his mission.

Variations in the daily lives of the occupants may go unnoticed in the documents but are readily visible in the archaeological record. For instance, forts often harbored civilians, including sutlers, women, children, and slaves, whose daily practices appear through the objects they left behind. Different foods prepared in different ways and served using different types of ceramics distinguished officers from soldiers at some sites, as did the size, location, contents, and construction materials of their quarters. Officers (perhaps at the urging of their wives) attempted to bring high culture to frontier life at some of the larger posts in Iowa through dinner parties, dances, theaters, and libraries along with churches and schools. Glass tumblers, etched glass serving dishes, and decorated ceramics suggest this type of refinement. At Fort Michilimackinac, officers lived in the northwest corner of the fortified area where they would afford themselves greater protection from cold northerly winter winds and be some distance from the hazardous powder magazine.

While many early forts had primarily defensive functions, they evolved to serve different purposes, as reflected in changing placements, size, spatial layout, and demographic composition. As Starbuck notes, frontier forts lost their efficacy during the Revolutionary War, which left behind encampments and other sites that reflected the faster movements of

American and British forces. Posts of the mid-nineteenth century west of the Mississippi River were intended to stop the encroachment of Euro-American settlers onto Indian lands and simultaneously police Indians at specific locations. Some fortifications facilitated political alliances by serving as nodes for exchange. Michigan's Fort St. Joseph supported a garrison of only 8–10 soldiers in the eighteenth century, yet it was an important commercial center for the distribution of imported goods that were traded for fur, skins, lead, tallow, and other resources acquired from the Indians.

Archaeology is well poised to contribute to the drama of conflict and hostility that has always accompanied warfare. Perhaps most poignant are the stories it reveals about the lives of ordinary soldiers ignored by history. At Valley Forge, Andersonville Prison, and various other military installations, archaeology underscores the rampant deprivation, boredom, and death that most men faced on a daily basis. Daily life for most soldiers at many of these sites was dull, full of endlessly repeated routines, drills, and patrols, with little chance for excitement. Soldiers sought to escape this monotony through drink, fight, and flight. Evidence for drinking has been found in the liquor bottles in officers' latrines at Fort Atkinson in Iowa. While some military sites are associated with famous Americans (George Washington at Fort Necessity) most were populated by average enlisted forces who probably yearned to see the end of conflict and a time when they would be reunited with loved ones. Harsh living conditions and starvation suggests that many soldiers experienced alienation.

Public interpretation of fort lifeways and battlefield activities can be presented through various means that involve primary documentary sources (e.g., maps, letters, and diaries), artifacts and other archaeological materials, and reconstructions with living history reenactors. While three-dimensional recreations are challenging to design and produce, they lend an air of realism that the public often finds compelling. At Fort Michilmackinac in Michigan, living history demonstrations have been featured in tandem with ongoing archaeological investigations for decades, much to public approval. Replicas of artifacts recovered from the site are employed in systemic context to show how they were actually used in the eighteenth century.

In addition to mundane artifacts and features, forts and battlefields often yield human remains. When those remains can be identified—or when living descendants are connected to the sites in question—the site may become a sacred place with heightened poignancy. As archaeologist Richard Gould reminds us, "recovery" under these conditions has a dual meaning that evokes both the retrieval of material remains and the restitution that follows from identification and subsequent reburial. Forts and battlefields are often seen as hallowed ground that can arouse great public controversy in the ways they are treated and commemorated. The sites of the Ludlow Massacre in Colorado and the World Trade Center in New York City are two immediate examples that come to mind.

Though military sites have been subject to investigation for decades, much of the work has been informed by the generally descriptive goals of the discipline in its infancy. Starbuck rightly notes that there are hundreds of fort and battlefield sites, and arguably thousands more if we look at conflict more broadly. Bomb shelters constructed during the Cold War can be considered in this category and subjected to archaeological scrutiny. These places of refuge were designed for personal protection in the event of nuclear warfare with our Communist enemies. Archaeology is well poised to identify the location as well as the design and any contents that these oftentimes clandestine sanctuaries may still hold. Foreign wars and even their mere threat had an impact on the material world of America, and the effect it has had on the American psyche is only beginning to be revealed. The numbers of dismembered veterans of our Iraq and Afghanistan wars are clear evidence of the trauma that we face. Archaeology can play a role in that trauma's catharsis.

Michael S. Nassaney
Series Editor

Preface and Acknowledgments

I never served in the military, but I have tremendous respect for those who do. Whether it be the protagonists of America's early wars, or those who serve in the Middle East today, I feel a great deal of admiration for the sacrifices made by soldiers and an equal measure of curiosity about life in the many short-term encampments that have housed men and women who are far from home and preparing to fight. Warfare is very satisfying to study, even though the reality of war is that soldiers too often experience deprivation, boredom, and death.

Many of those who specialize in the field of historical archaeology have conducted excavations at military sites, and a single volume can barely do justice to all of our efforts. Still, I would like to thank the many archaeologists whose research projects on military sites have made this book possible. Dick Ping Hsu, retired National Park Service archaeologist for the North Atlantic Region, first invited me to commence excavations at Saratoga National Historical Park (the Saratoga Battlefield) in 1985. Dick had excavated Fort Stanwix some fifteen years earlier, and thanks to his initial prompting, I have now had the pleasure of excavating, and learning from, military sites in the northeastern United States for the past twenty-five years.

I would also like to thank Douglas Scott (retired, National Park Service), David Orr (Temple University), Larry Babits (East Carolina University), Timothy J. Todish, Merle Parsons, Matthew Rozell, Dennis Howe, Gordon and Barbara De Angelo, Daniel Sivilich, Brad Jarvis, Andy Farry, Elizabeth Hall, Maureen Kennedy, June Talley, John Farrell, Sarah Majot, Linda White, and the hundreds of other colleagues, friends, volunteers, and students who have advised or worked with me over the years while excavating eighteenth-century military sites. Their efforts in the field and the laboratory have added greatly to our knowledge of military sites archaeology and have contributed immeasurably to the preparation of this book.

I have included case studies from several time periods and diverse regions of the United States, but admittedly this book cannot be all-inclusive. Rather, my intention is to blend appropriate research questions with exciting field projects and up-to-date analytical techniques so that the reader will fully appreciate how rewarding military sites archaeology has become.

Finally, thanks are due to Michael Nassaney, editor for the series The American Experience in Archaeological Perspective, and the staff of the University Press of Florida for their help in bringing this book to completion. Their patience during the preparation of this volume has been exceptional.

1

An Archaeologist's Perspective

Is war an inevitable part of the human experience? Perhaps. But no matter how many studies have been done of forts, battlefields, and battle strategies, it is always possible to learn more, and the use of archaeology has long proven to be one of the best ways to better understand America's military conflicts. This volume explores some of the questions archaeologists ask when studying military sites, some of the techniques used for locating and documenting forts and battlefields, and some of the more interesting and provocative findings (see figure 1.1). This clearly is an enormous topic. (See *The Archaeology of War*, 2005, for a rich selection of battle sites from all over the world and Arkush and Allen 2006 for theoretical perspectives on early warfare.)

Archaeology Conducted at Military Sites

The current fascination with military sites archaeology is nothing new. Even before systematic excavations began in the 1930s, there was no lack of artifact collectors and scavengers who acquired souvenirs after each of America's major conflicts. In fact, the surface collecting of every battlefield goes back almost to the moment of actual conflict. Some of the best early work was conducted by William Louis Calver and Reginald Pelham Bolton between 1918 and about 1937 as they collected artifacts and conducted small excavations in the greater New York area (Calver and Bolton 1950; summarized in Starbuck 1999a). Their systematic, published descriptions of the artifacts they found at sites such as the Dyckman Farm in Manhattan really mark the beginning of military sites archaeology as we know it today. In more modern times, as training and methods have improved, military sites have probably received more attention from archaeologists in the United States than any other category of historical site,

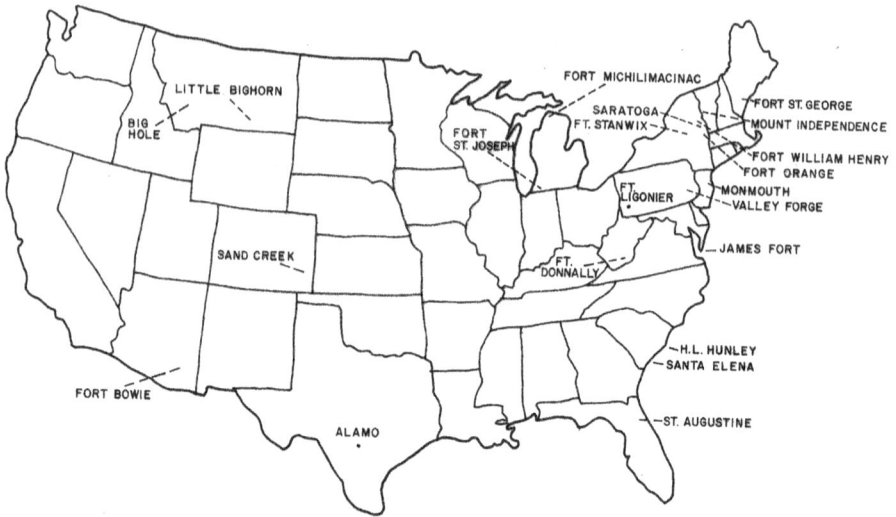

Figure 1.1. Some of the key military sites in the United States.

and this may be equally true all over the world. There is an enormous body of literature that pertains specifically to the history and organization of military sites, and there are many specialized types of military construction (barracks, magazines, blockhouses, earthworks, moats, and more) that need to be understood in order to effectively conduct military sites archaeology (Campbell 1967). However, it is in the questions asked—and answered—that military sites archaeology has been able to go well beyond the simple artifact descriptions of Calver and Bolton.

Every nation has fascinating military sites, whether the 2,000-year-old remains of the Battle of the Teutoberg Forest, where 20,000 Roman soldiers were annihilated by Germanic warriors (Wells 2003), or Fortress Louisbourg on Cape Breton Island in Nova Scotia, which offered protection to the French fishing fleet (construction began in 1719), or the 1746 Culloden Battlefield in Scotland (Pollard 2009), or World War I battlefields in France, or the 1836 Battle of the Alamo in San Antonio, Texas (figure 1.2), or any of thousands of other points of conflict. But how scholars have approached these sites has differed greatly, and the number of instances of "pure" research has been greatly outnumbered by digs that have used archaeology as a precursor to restoration or reconstruction. After all, the quality of historic site interpretation has almost always been improved through the use of archaeological techniques, and nearly every historic fort or battlefield that is interpreted to the public has relied upon archaeology at some point to determine the footprint of elusive features such as hut sites, roadways, and embankments; trace the movements of combatants across open terrain; or tell the stories of ordinary soldiers' lives.

This book begins with a review of some of the research questions and techniques that are appropriate to military sites archaeology, and then proceeds to describe some of the earliest sixteenth- and seventeenth-century forts that were built in the American colonies, specifically those that have been rediscovered by archaeologists. I have then selected four major conflicts in American history—the French and Indian War, the American Revolution, the Civil War, and Indian Wars in the American West—to illustrate the contribution of archaeology to the study of forts and battlefields and their role in shaping the American experience. For each of these wars my goal is to demonstrate how archaeology has been able to go beyond traditional histories, sometimes refuting "common wisdom" but always adding color and a "you are there" perspective. A generalized overview of each war and some of its sites of conflict is followed by a detailed case study. Fort William Henry, location of the 1757 massacre described in *The Last of the Mohicans* (Cooper 1826), will be used to exemplify archaeology at a site of the French and Indian War. Mount

Figure 1.2. The Alamo as it appears today in San Antonio, Texas.

Figure 1.3. Military sites in the northeastern United States.

Independence, perhaps the most intact large military site of the 1770s, will represent the American Revolution. The 1864 Confederate submarine *H. L. Hunley* will exemplify the American Civil War. Finally, the 1876 Battle of the Little Bighorn will demonstrate how battlefield archaeology has been conducted in the American West.

While I have tried to include examples of many types of military sites, I must apologize in advance for not being able to include many other forts and battlefields and for giving minimal coverage to some conflicts, such as the War of 1812 and the Mexican-American War. There simply are too many significant military sites. Hundreds of forts have already been excavated, and battlefield studies, also referred to as "conflict studies" by Douglas Scott (personal communication, Jan. 9, 2009), are ongoing at such far-flung battlefields as the River Raisin Battlefield in Michigan (War of 1812), the San Jacinto Battlefield in Texas (Mexican-American War), and sites all over Florida from the Seminole Wars of the 1830s. However, this book is not intended to be encyclopedic in its coverage, and instead I will select examples of excavations from several points in time and use them to highlight some of the research questions and some of the successes that have come from military sites archaeology. My own research is most often focused upon the northeastern United States, and that region has an especially large number of military sites (figure 1.3).

How Have Military Sites Helped to Shape America's National Image?

The "action" that took place at forts and battlefields has helped to define America, and there is a great deal of national pride invested in every one of these sites. They embody activities and locations where opposing nations and cultures came into conflict and where victory or defeat helped to shape our nation as we know it today. The French and Indian War determined that we would be an English-speaking nation with a strong tradition in British law and custom. The American Revolution separated us from our colonial overlord and gave us the potential for greatness as a free and independent nation. The Civil War held our country together as a nation at a time when slavery and regional differences could have split us apart into smaller, lesser nations. And clearly the Indian Wars in the American West were a terrible and regrettable clash of cultures, with western expansion by those of European descent leading to the cultural destruction of many indigenous peoples.

While all of these events and processes have been summarized by historians in traditional history textbooks, long-ago events have the potential to feel very remote to those living today. The dates for military campaigns and the names of commanders may appear to be facts to be memorized, with no greater significance. That is why archaeology has enormous potential to connect us with the past and to bring relevance and excitement. Visitors are able to walk through the ruins of past conflicts, view accurate reconstructions of fortifications, and touch or at least observe the objects

Figure 1.4. A reenactor portraying an officer from the French and Indian War. Fort Edward, New York, September 2006.

left behind by the warriors of earlier generations. With good archaeological interpretation, the objects *do* "speak" and provide a firsthand experience to those who visit a Gettysburg Battlefield, a Fort Ticonderoga, or a Confederate submarine in a tank of water in Charleston, South Carolina.

With all deference to my history colleagues, I have had far too many people tell me that they always found history to be boring in school but the moment they stepped foot on a battlefield, the past suddenly came alive. They were able to visualize how events had taken place and they could imagine how commanders had formulated their strategies. Archaeology provides a necessary link with ordinary people, with extraordinary events, and with all of the very tangible artifacts, stains, and features they left behind. Historical reenactors provide a very similar experience, for they too seek to bring relevance to the past (figure 1.4).

The Problem with Collectors and Dealers in Military Artifacts

Military artifacts often have a high monetary value, and the fringes of famed battlefields are under constant attack by those who wish to "own" a piece of history for themselves. Even state or federally owned sites cannot be monitored every moment, and penalties tend to be weak for those caught in the act of looting. This contrasts with the goals of professional archaeology which strives to ask good research questions, using the most up-to-date techniques to locate and record artifacts, features, and their context. Archaeology requires that we accurately identify finds and properly conserve them, systematically write up the results, and then place everything—artifacts and records—in public repositories where others may examine them and draw their own conclusions. By definition, treasure hunters do not do this, and the shortcuts they employ leave little for future generations to study. Collectors have gone to extraordinary lengths to tear apart Civil War battlefields, in particular, as they look for saleable artifacts. Unfortunately, these are nonrenewable resources, and no site can withstand repeated looting.

I have had treasure hunters brag to me that they are more successful at finding military sites and artifacts than archaeologists are. While sometimes that may be true, if the best possible field and laboratory methods cannot be brought to bear, followed by thorough publication of results, then the site should be avoided altogether. It is not a contest to see who can find the most. As an example of what happens all too often, some years ago my telephone rang at about 5:00 a.m., I answered it, and an older male voice said, "My name is Tom Jones, and I've been digging a blockhouse site just south of Fort Edward [New York]. Would you like to see what I've been finding?" I cautiously said, "Okay," agreeing to meet him at a somewhat later time that morning.

When I subsequently saw his rusty pickup truck, with artifacts scattered across the bed, I knew that I was in for a bit of an adventure. What followed was a trip to a pothole-riddled bluff overlooking the Hudson River. In the grass around each looter's hole was a scattering of artifacts and butchered bones—the discarded finds that would bring little money on the antiquities market. As I looked at my new collector-friend, who was eagerly awaiting my approval (I think I was supposed to say, "My, you *are* a great archaeologist!"), it was clear that our only common ground was our mutual love of history. There are a finite number of military sites that are still able to reveal information, many have been seriously disturbed already, and each one deserves the best, the most professional documentation it can get.

I am also reminded of the experience of a law enforcement colleague of mine, then the senior park ranger at Saratoga National Historical Park. He and a fellow ranger came upon two collectors in army fatigues shoveling as fast as they could go through artifact deposits from the Battle of Saratoga (1777). The two rangers crept through the woods with guns drawn, caught the perpetrators in the act, and heard the standard litany: "We didn't know this was wrong, officer!" Their metal detectors and motor vehicle were confiscated and held as evidence, and a subsequent check at other National Park sites revealed that the same fellows had previously been caught elsewhere. The case was presented to the county district attorney, but the market value of the artifacts they had uncovered was fairly low, so it was difficult to bring the case to court.

Unfortunately, serious penalties are rarely imposed. Only if the penalty for collecting from military sites includes serious jail time is there a chance that looting can be reduced. After all, if a single military button can be sold on the Internet for $200 or more, then the confiscation of a metal detector is not likely to have much effect. The past must be shared and managed by all so that all may benefit. Most important, artifacts need to be stored and displayed in secure, climate-controlled facilities where scholars and the visiting public will all have a chance to learn and enjoy.

In the chapters that follow, we will be looking at examples of what constitutes careful military sites archaeology. With well-thought-out research questions, appropriate methodologies, systematic field and laboratory techniques, and the preparation of comprehensive reports when we're done, America's military sites will have many new stories to tell us.

2

Research Priorities

Why dig military sites? What can we hope to learn that is not already known through rigorous historical research? Didn't military engineers prepare measured drawings showing every structure of significance? Haven't enough military books been written already?

I occasionally hear these questions and others, and I would like to paraphrase the critique of an anonymous book reviewer that was sent to me years ago: "This archaeology [at a fort on Lake Champlain] is only of local interest. . . . If you want to write a book, perhaps you could do a reassessment of the strategies behind one of the major battles." This assessment by an historian misinterprets what military site archaeologists do. Our field has long since lost its preoccupation with digging and restoring forts, and we certainly do not want to conduct the umpteenth armchair analysis of the motives behind a particular battle.

Rather, modern archaeology is very much a study of the lives of ordinary soldiers and officers, and this includes an examination of all of the evidence that archaeology can provide for class and regional distinctions. We seek to understand the complexities of provisioning and consumption patterns as well as to determine how soldiers and engineers constructed earthworks, palisades, and even makeshift shelters. How did they feed themselves? Did they take personal keepsakes from home to their camps on the frontier? Was everything "standard military issue"? This shifting of research priorities no doubt began during the processual archaeology of the 1960s and has continued with the appearance of critical theory and other, "newer" archaeologies. It is safe to say that my anonymous book reviewer still subscribed to the "famous person, famous event" approach to history, but this has been rejected by most scholars and replaced by the more inclusive approaches of modern social historians and archaeologists.

In considering research questions and priorities, there are several categories of military sites, and each presents its own questions and difficulties in interpretation. Most conspicuous are the remains of forts, whether the more permanent masonry forts along the Atlantic seaboard or the small, interior, log forts that consisted of little more than a few palisade walls. Many of the forts were surrounded by earthworks or entrenchments that were far more extensive than the fort itself, so each fort was often the centerpiece of an enormous, sprawling complex of military architecture. To these substantial constructions may be added the many fortified houses (garrison houses) and blockhouses that are located just about everywhere. Such houses were often built "just a little bit stronger" to ward off Indian attacks.

The greatest numbers of forts were built during the earliest years of settlement, the period leading up to and including the French and Indian War, when every town had at least one fort for mutual defense plus occasional blockhouses or garrison houses. Fewer forts were built during the American Revolution, and even fewer during the short-lived War of 1812. The Civil War resulted in some additional fort construction, especially along the Atlantic Coast, and expansion into the American West prompted a great deal of fort building on the western frontier. In general, forts have left behind prominent structural remains, and because they make for dramatic public exhibits, dozens of forts have been reconstructed.

Most forts have been interpreted for public viewing by using a combination of original engineers' drawings and archaeological excavation. A few, however, were reconstructed before the existence of professional archaeology, and thus some of the earliest fort reconstructions are not very accurate. Archaeology, after all, means more than simply picking up the artifacts that have been disturbed as the stone masons are rebuilding everything in sight. Early-twentieth-century reconstructions that gave priority to period engineers' drawings, without the use of archaeology, sometimes created very inaccurate "monuments to the past" because they reflected what early engineers *planned* to build and not what they *actually* built. At a prominent reconstructed fort of the French and Indian War in northern New York state, for example, the main gate was inaccurately rebuilt precisely because early-twentieth-century builders did not know how to use archaeology during their reconstruction process.

Very different are the many battlefields where conflict often raged for no more than a few hours, leaving behind a scatter of artifacts and a

Figure 2.1. Metal detecting at the Monmouth Battlefield in New Jersey. Here members of BRAVO are systematically walking the surface of the field, flagging musket balls and other metal artifacts.

patterning of activities so thin that it would seem almost impossible to extract any information from the soil. However, it is in the area of battlefield archaeology where some of the most recent technological and methodological advances have occurred, and the use of metal detectors and more sophisticated remote sensing equipment have added many new insights into battle strategies and maneuvers. Whether it is the Monmouth Battlefield (figure 2.1), or the Little Bighorn, Saratoga, Yorktown, or Gettysburg, battlefields have received almost as much attention as forts.

Just as important for modern research are the enormous military encampment sites that have survived from all wars, providing us with a detailed look at aspects of provisioning, architecture, camp layout, and daily activities that were shared by thousands of soldiers and officers. Did the soldiers live in rows of huts, tents, or tents with boards added to make them more permanent (i.e., winterized)? Or did they live in massive barracks buildings? The shelters and lifestyles of ordinary soldiers is a topic that can never receive enough attention from scholars, and the study of camp life has to be the fastest-growing specialty within military sites archaeology. (Civil War huts especially come to mind; see Geier, Orr, and Reeves 2006.) My own research has long focused upon encampments, and these small settlements far from home were important settings in which American concepts of freedom and innovation were able to grow. Encampment sites also provide some of the best opportunities for future research because, while many forts and battlefields were dug or reconstructed before the existence of good recording techniques, encampments have often been overlooked and so have managed to retain more of their integrity.

Research Questions Appropriate to Military Sites Archaeology

Military sites archaeology prompts a variety of research questions. No matter what the time period or setting, we archaeologists especially like to examine the differences between expected behavior and actual behavior. For example, were there observable differences in living standards between officers and enlisted men, or did service on the frontier, far from home, have a noticeable leveling effect? Were camp layouts, techniques of fort construction, and standards of cleanliness all based on guidelines rigidly laid out in military manuals, or did soldiers and engineers—when far from home—tend to improvise and use less rigorous or more vernacular approaches to organizing their lives? In other words, were European models modified and adapted to the American landscape and were new construction techniques developed that took advantage of local materials and local know-how?

Can archaeology be used to differentiate among the diverse ethnic, racial, and regional backgrounds that typified soldiers and officers? And to what extent do artifacts really differ within an encampment of soldiers? If most provisioning came from the same suppliers or sutlers, then wouldn't all individuals within a camp pretty much share the same material culture? That may sometimes have been true, but we do occasionally find evidence for more "personal" artifacts, brought from home, that may provide insights into a soldier's background.

Was all material culture outdated at military outposts? In other words, is archaeology able to demonstrate a lag effect from urban centers to the frontier? Were soldiers the last to receive the latest manufactures from the Atlantic seaboard or from Europe, and did they even care? Were soldiers actually aware of the latest weapons, fashions, or innovations?

Is archaeology able to show whether food consumed by the army was fresh or dried, wild or domestic? Did armies chiefly consume salted pork and beef, as described in orderly books, or was there an eagerness to seek out sources of fresh vegetables and live animals (fresh meat) at every opportunity? To what extent were wild game, fish, and shellfish used to supplement standard military rations? Was there danger from enemy combatants when soldiers left camp, seeking out wild sources of food, and was it harmful to discipline when soldiers sought to augment their regular rations this way?

Can archaeology be used to discover the military roads and paths by which armies traveled (e.g., Kingsley 1997)? Can the very thoroughfares used by armies be located and identified by examining ruts or artifact scatters? After all, for armies that were always on the move, a big part of their story is the "getting there" part. And what determined where a particular fort or battlefield was sited? Was it elevation, soil drainage, proximity to water, or the availability of some other resource yet to be determined?

Above all, is archaeology able to tell interesting stories about the ordinary soldiers who have too often been ignored by history? This is perhaps the greatest objective for military sites archaeology today, and for all of historical archaeology, because our ability to connect with the past is best achieved when we identify with ordinary people—the who and why of every military camp. "Standard" issue, "routine" ways of doing things, are stated or implied through historical sources, but understanding what armies actually did often requires the application of archaeological methods.

Sampling and Deciding Where to Dig

How does one sample a fort, a battlefield, or an encampment? Some of my colleagues have told me that it is sufficient to excavate only one out of a row of huts, or just one example out of any category of cultural feature. Others have argued that it is preferable to dig no more than 5 or 10 percent of any given site. This logic states that we must leave most of what we find intact and in the ground, awaiting the better techniques that will be developed someday. While this may sound like a valid preservationist approach, in many cases a small sample size really accomplishes very little. Retrieving a 5 percent sample of artifacts, or digging one building out of ten, will not reveal the incredible diversity of activities, social hierarchies (class), or evidence of seasonality that may exist throughout a military

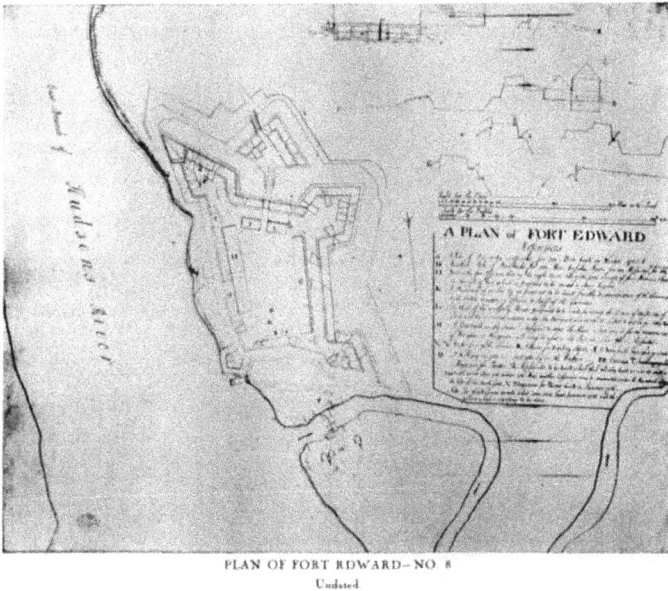

Figure 2.2. A plan of Fort Edward in 1756. This detailed engineer's drawing depicts Fort Edward on the east bank of the Hudson River, and the legend identifies the various structures on the plan. There is no guarantee of accuracy because engineers sometimes did not even visit the sites they were drawing. Crown Collection of Photographs of American Maps, New York State Library.

camp. And testing only a small percentage of a structure will probably not reveal doorways, windows, fireplaces, or processing areas. Rather, a limited artifact sample—not capable of revealing structural information—is little better than systematic treasure hunting in what it is able to achieve. Statistical sampling means little unless most categories of features are located and sampled.

Every project must begin with a thorough analysis of primary documents, engineers' maps (figure 2.2), and high-resolution aerial photographs, followed by pedestrian surveys and interviews with property owners and assorted informants. Systematic metal-detector surveys and other types of remote sensing will further aid in narrowing down the area to be sampled, and then test pits or trenches can be placed according to how extensive—or intensive—the research objectives are. If approaching an earthwork, a simple trench or two placed at right angles to the feature will provide an adequate cross-section of soil layers and reveal the construction sequence. On the other hand, if a hut or tent site is being examined to determine season of occupation or to establish whether the occupant (or occupants) was an officer or group of soldiers, then test pits might need to expose a majority of the site before there is clear evidence of windows and doorways, a fireplace, or artifacts that might reveal the status of the occupant(s).

Given the very substantial structural remains that survive at many military sites, ground-penetrating radar, proton magnetometry and electrical resistivity surveys have all proven effective, and the geophysical surveys have become essential to developing good excavation strategies. For example, soil resistivity surveys have been used with considerable success at Fort Michilimackinac (Williams and Shapiro 1982), Fort Riley in Kansas (Hargrave et al. 2002), and Fort St. Joseph in Michigan (Nassaney, Cremin, and Lynch 2002–2004). Depending upon available funding, it is often desirable to choose multiple geophysical survey techniques, and at Fort St. Joseph, ground-penetrating radar and magnetometry proved even more successful than electrical resistivity. On the other hand, there are some testing strategies that accomplish very little at military sites. Placing shovel test pits at regular intervals across the surface of a battlefield will reveal almost no information of value, and placing a 1-×-1-m test pit inside a hut or an earthwork will merely collect a small artifact sample, not provide structural or functional information.

It thus is critical that military sites archaeologists select strategies and techniques that are best suited to answering the project's research questions. In the same sense that there are many categories of military sites, there are also many approaches to choose from. Shovel tests, ground-penetrating radar, and predictive modeling are not *de rigueur* at every site. It also is not possible to answer questions about social stratification, provisioning, or trade with Native Americans at every site. Rather, what *is* critical is that the military sites archaeologist be well aware of all the options available and then select methodologies that have a reasonable chance of success. The extremely effective use of metal detectors at the Little Bighorn and Monmouth battlefields, for example, was the result of applying existing technology in innovative ways to answer very old questions about troop movements. Sometimes "thinking outside the box" really does work.

3

Forts and Battlefields: Sixteenth- and Seventeenth-Century Beginnings

The earliest European settlements in the Americas invariably were protected by forts, reflecting hostilities among rival European nations as well as the threat of attack by Native Americans who were rapidly being displaced. Fort designs were indicative of what was familiar to military engineers based on European antecedents, but they also reflected the construction materials that were available locally, and they needed to be put up quickly. In a few cases, they may have represented a "borrowing" from the designs of native palisaded fortifications. Many of the designs created by military engineers had previously been successful in Europe (Robinson 1977), although numerous modifications were no doubt made once construction was underway here in the colonies. Archaeology thus becomes the only accurate guide to the appearance of many early forts because the engineers' drawings that have survived in the historical record may not reflect what was actually built.

Many of the forts in the Northeast were constructed to separate the British from the French colonies, whereas others separated the French from the Spanish in the Southeast. None of the short-term forts of the earliest settlers has survived in an intact condition. Later masonry forts have survived far better, but wood fortifications invariably exist today only as patterns of posthole stains and trenches. Still, simple period sketches coupled with archaeological remains can be immensely helpful for the interpretation of early fort design.

Over the past 30 years, our knowledge of fort construction during the period of initial European contact has grown enormously, thanks to the discovery of the English fort at Martin's Hundred in Virginia, the Spanish fort of Santa Elena on Parris Island in South Carolina, and, most recently, the discovery of James Fort on the James River in Virginia and Fort St. George at the mouth of the Kennebec River in Maine. All have been published on extensively, and James Fort has the added virtue of being available for public viewing.

Spanish Forts

St. Augustine, Florida, was founded in 1565 as the first permanent European settlement within what is now the United States. Beginning that same year, there were a series of short-lived wooden forts in the St. Augustine area, but none of these has been located or excavated. Each was intended to resist threats from French colonists to the north or from Timucua Indians who already lived on Florida's northeastern coast (Chaney and Deagan 1989). It is the later forts of St. Augustine that have survived and been intensively excavated and restored, most notably the Castillo de San Marcos, begun in 1672 and with walls built of coquina block (Arana and Manucy 2005). The Castillo was built by Spain because of raids by English pirates, and it was equipped with seagates that would flood the otherwise-dry moat if they were attacked. Florida, and specifically St. Augustine, was Spain's primary military base from 1565 until 1763, at which time the British took over the site.

Just to the north, in 1566 Spain constructed a fort at the southern tip of what is now Parris Island in South Carolina, hoping to protect the Spanish colonial city of Santa Elena from the French and Indians. Santa Elena was substantial enough to have 60 houses and a maximum population of 400, but when Sir Francis Drake attacked St. Augustine in 1587, the Spanish settlers went to St. Augustine's aid and never returned. Three forts had been created during the short period of residence: San Felipe I (1566–70), San Felipe II (1570–76), and Fort San Marcos (1577–87). Santa Elena occasionally saw digging over the years, but Stanley South of the Institute of Archaeology and Anthropology at the University of South Carolina conducted the first professional excavation here from 1979 to 1985 (and again after 1991) into what is now the Parris Island Marine Corps golf course.

South and his team have found bits of fire-baked mud (all that was left of the Spanish houses), sixteenth-century Spanish pottery, and a moat that measured 14 ft wide and 5 ft deep, most likely the moat that surrounded Fort San Felipe II from 1574 to 1576 (South 1979; Judge 1988). South has made many important finds at Santa Elena, but of special interest are the equal proportions of European-made and Indian-made artifacts, revealing that Europeans were borrowing heavily from the local Native American population.

British Forts

English explorers led by Sir Walter Raleigh landed on Roanoke Island in 1584 and attempted to colonize what is now North Carolina. When they constructed Fort Raleigh in 1585, this became the first British fort in the colonies, now encompassed within Fort Raleigh National Historic Site. Many years later, when J. C. Harrington commenced excavations here for the National Park Service in 1947, no one knew conclusively where the fort had been located, but Harrington successfully located remains from the fort on a low rise of ground (Harrington 1962).

Few American historical sites have attracted as much interest as Jamestown, site of the first English settlement on the James River in Virginia and founded in 1607 by about 108 men and boys. While the location of the town of Jamestown has always been known, the location of its early fort, James Fort, eluded the National Park Service archaeologists who excavated there in the 1930s and the 1950s (Cotter 1958). It was generally assumed that the fort, built in just 19 days, had washed into the James River, and all recent site maps were drawn with the fort placed a short distance out into the river. Thus it was a truly exceptional discovery when William Kelso, employed by the Association for the Preservation of Virginia Antiquities, discovered the still-intact footprint of the fort on the shore of the James River in 1994 (Kelso 1993, 1995–2001, 2006).

Kelso was working alone when he exposed the first palisade trench, and his crew has grown substantially since then. Only a single corner bulwark of the triangular fort had eroded into the river, and to date all three palisade wall trenches and two of the corner bulwarks have been exposed (figure 3.1), as well as edge weapons, cabasset helmets and breastplates, a sixteenth-century Scottish snaphaunce pistol lock, an ivory compass, and more than 500,000 objects. Historical documents indicate that a church, several buildings, and a well were inside the fort. Kelso's team has now discovered and excavated that well, recorded forever by an overhead camera that automatically photographed the excavation every ten minutes (figure 3.2).

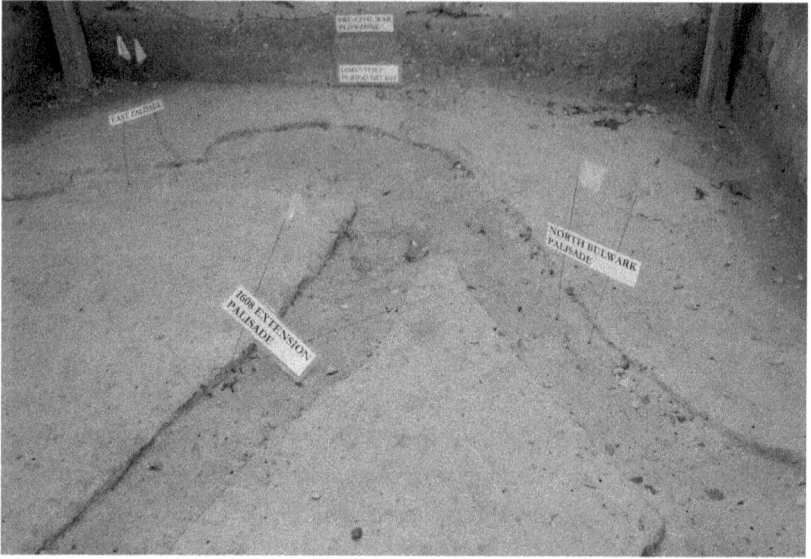

Figure 3.1. Palisade trenches at James Fort, November 2005.

Figure 3.2. The ongoing excavation of James Fort in November 2005. William Kelso (*with hat*) stands just to the right of the total station, and the camera boom that continuously recorded the excavation appears at the top right.

While Jamestown (and James Fort) is commonly referred to as "the first permanent English settlement in America," there was a contemporary, albeit short-lived, English settlement on the coast of Maine. The 100 or so colonists who made up the Popham Colony, named after George Popham, left Plymouth, England, in two ships only a few months after those sent out from London to found the Jamestown Colony. Upon reaching the Sagadahoc (Kennebec) River in Maine, their first order of business was to commence construction of Fort St. George on August 20, 1607. A superb, although probably exaggerated, map of Fort St. George was prepared by a military cartographer, John Hunt, on October 8, 1607, and the Hunt map shows "a completely finished fort with nine cannons, battlemented gates (emblazoned with flags and pennants), and at least 25 structures within the compound" (Brain 2007: 12; the map appears in Brain 2007: 10–11).

Given the very short time that had passed, it is difficult to imagine a small group of settlers accomplishing that much in just seven weeks, and the only building inside the fort that appeared certain was a large storehouse into which the two ships needed to unload their supplies before they returned to England. It was perhaps an omen of what was to come when a shortage of supplies caused half of the colonists to return to England that fall; soon after, the death of George Popham on February 5, 1608, prompted the rest of the colonists to abandon the colony for good in the fall of 1608.

Jeffrey Brain knew most of these historical details when he commenced his search for Fort St. George in 1994, and as he continued field work between 1997 and 2005, Brain excavated much of the storehouse and many other features inside the fort (Brain 1995, 1997, 1998, 1999, 2000, 2001, 2007). In doing so, he discovered that the storehouse was a solid, well-built structure, but that most of the settlers lived in "little more than rude huts" (Brain 2007: 153). The one exception was the house of Raleigh Gilbert, the second in command (behind George Popham), whose burned house contained by far the finest artifacts to be found in Popham Colony.

Only slightly later in time is the site of Martin's Hundred, some ten miles up the James River from Jamestown, Virginia. In 1976 archaeologists from Colonial Williamsburg were at work within Carter's Grove Plantation when they encountered early-seventeenth-century graves. As Colonial Williamsburg's director of archaeology, Ivor Noël Hume, checked the historical literature, he realized they had discovered the remains of the long-lost community of Wolstenholme Towne, first occupied in 1619 by about 220 settlers. Further research revealed that the community of Martin's Hundred had been sent to Virginia by the Virginia Company of London, but sadly the town they created came to a tragic end on March 22, 1622, when 78 out of 140 inhabitants were massacred by Indians. Some of those who escaped were to return in 1623, but virtually everyone was gone by the 1650s, and the location of Wolstenholme Towne was forgotten. As excavations began, Noël Hume gradually exposed the complete ground plan of a timber fort that was trapezoidal in outline (and which he termed "Site C").

Prior to the 1994 discovery of James Fort, the fort at Martin's Hundred provided the earliest complete ground plan known for any British colonial wooden fort, and this was exposed in its entirety. The fort at Martin's Hundred had posts set 9 ft apart, probably with rails and planks in-between the posts, and the fort enclosed an area of about 10,000 ft^2. There even were four postholes that suggested a square watchtower inside the enclosure. Several years of research by Noël Hume revealed parts from five matchlock muskets, powder flasks, swords, plate armor, and two close helmets. At the time, these were the only close helmets that had ever been excavated in the New World, and they dated to the sixteenth and early seventeenth centuries, suggesting that these settlers had been sent to the colonies with quite antiquated weapons (Noël Hume 1994; Noël Hume and Noël Hume 2001). Unfortunately, the armor and other weapons did them little good when Indians entered their homes on the morning of March 22, 1622.

French Forts

Facing conflict with Spanish settlements just to the south, an expedition of 150 French Protestants constructed Charlesfort in 1562 on the southern tip of Parris Island, South Carolina. Facing starvation, they left just a year later, and after another four years Spanish forces arrived and built their own fort of San Felipe over the top of the old fort. Stanley South has been exploring both the early French settlement here as well as the later Spanish forts.

Soon afterward (1564), about 200 French settlers also built Fort Caroline near what is now Jacksonville, Florida, where a scaled-down reconstruction of the fort is open to the public as Fort Caroline National Memorial. Unfortunately, Fort Caroline attracted the attention of Spain, the garrison was captured, and 132 French male settlers were executed. After only a year, Fort Caroline was destroyed. The site of Fort Caroline has not yet been discovered, but archaeologists are actively seeking it (Rose 2005).

An excellent example of research at a later seventeenth-century French fort is the work of Alaric Faulkner at Fort Pentagoet in Castine, Maine. Occupied between 1635 and 1674, Fort Pentagoet was part of French Acadia at a time when half the coast of Maine was claimed by France. Pentagoet's role was to protect Acadian settlements in northern Maine while serving as a trading post for multiple cultures, including even the English. Although this site had considerable economic importance, it could not survive being burned and leveled by Flemish captain Jurriaen Aernouts in 1674.

Recognizing the enormous potential of this site, Faulkner, of the University of Maine at Orono, excavated at Fort Pentagoet from 1981 to 1984 inside the Barracks and Commandant's Quarters (Faulkner 1981, 1986; Faulkner and Faulkner 1987). In doing so he discovered that the archaeological remains have great integrity, with a rich armorer's workshop, good preservation of organic materials, and excellent evidence for the "French" presence in the American colonies.

Dutch Forts

Fort Orange was built by the Dutch West India Company in 1624 on the west bank of the Hudson River in what later became Albany, New York. It was constructed with four bastions on the edge of the river, with the two eastern bastions on the riverbank and with a moat surrounding the fort on the other three sides. It operated as an important center for the fur trade until 1664, when the English took over control of the fort from the Dutch. The English renamed it Fort Albany but allowed it to deteriorate until they abandoned it in 1676, even as they built a new Fort Albany nearby. Still later, as the city of Albany began to expand in about 1790, Broadway Street was constructed across the two eastern bastions of the fort. Simeon DeWitt, the surveyor-general for New York State, then built a large mansion (50 ft on a side) on top of the interior of the fort, destroying much of what was left, and he often boasted that he was living atop Fort Orange.

The fort was thus incorporated into the modern city of Albany and remained hidden until 1970, when Paul Huey, as he studied early maps of the area, discovered that a highway (Interstate 787) was about to go through the remains of the fort. Huey conducted an emergency excavation here from October 1970 until March 1971, initially using a backhoe to look for undisturbed deposits. This was a difficult excavation because of the many eighteenth- and nineteenth-century intrusions, but in the process he found Dutch artifacts everywhere, including sherds of tin-glazed earthenware, fine German stoneware, trade beads, wampum (used as currency), clay tobacco pipes (pipe stems were often reworked into whistles), and even elegant decorated glassware from the Rhine Valley in Holland (Huey 1988, 1991, 1998). One of Huey's primary conclusions, based on the richness of the finds, was that employees of the Dutch West India Company had been importing European goods of high quality out to the frontier of colonial America: "No effort was spared in the importation of the rich material culture of this period and in reestablishing the comfort and sophistication of everyday life in the Netherlands" (Huey 1991: 61).

Fort Orange was easily the most significant Dutch fort to be constructed in seventeenth-century America, and its remains rest at the center of the lively Dutch scholarship that continues in the Albany area today.

Final Thoughts

Historical archaeology has been extremely effective in demonstrating the great diversity in building styles and material culture—and, perhaps, even the aspirations—of the different nations that were colonizing the New World. The early Spanish, English, French, and Dutch settlements had differing goals and approaches to dealing with frontier settings, and as they contested with native populations and with each other, they left behind a rich legacy of forts, palisades, battlefields, dumps, wells, and settlements. Early Spanish fortifications tended to be somewhat more massive, permanent, and coastal—built to protect them from French and British attack in the Southeast—whereas forts built by the other nations were relatively ephemeral and often used for a single campaign or to protect local trade. Many of these fort sites have been destroyed or built over, but for those that still have physical remains, such as James Fort, it is truly exciting for the public to be able to "share in the adventure" as early forts are unearthed today.

4

The French and Indian War

The several wars that led up to the French and Indian War (1754–63), or Seven Years' War, embodied a worldwide struggle between France and England for control of land and resources (Anderson 2000, 2005; Rose 2005). These earlier wars included King William's War (1689–1697), Queen Anne's War (1701–13), and King George's War (1744–48). Schenectady, New York, was attacked and destroyed during King William's War in 1690, and Deerfield, Massachusetts, was attacked and razed during what has become known as the "1704 raid on Deerfield," as were many other settlements throughout New England. English settlers were carried off to Canada as captives throughout this period, and in turn, the English and their Mohawk allies attacked Canada. Intermittent raids, followed by periods of peace, continued until 1763, when the English finally conquered Canada for good.

Sites from the earliest conflicts have seen relatively little archaeology. However, by the 1750s, an all-out struggle between England and France resulted in the creation of numerous forts, battlefields, and trading posts that *have* left substantial archaeological remains. Notable among these were two Pennsylvania battle sites: the 1754 Battle of Great Meadows (the Battle of Fort Necessity), in which General George Washington and a regiment of Virginians were forced to surrender to a superior French force, and the 1755 Battle of the Wilderness (Braddock's Defeat), in which the French destroyed a British column and Major General Edward Braddock was mortally wounded.

Further to the north, the Battle of Lake George followed in September 1755, and this time the French lost to a British force under General William Johnson; soon after, the British surrendered two forts at Oswego, New York, in 1756. Thousands of British soldiers subsequently fought outside the walls of Fort Ticonderoga in northern New York state in 1758 and

1759; during just the attack in 1758, they lost 1,900 men. Finally, at the end of this contentious period, the British were firmly in control, and when the Treaty of Paris was signed in 1763, France lost its claims to much of the New World. France later regained the so-called Louisiana Territory from Spain in exchange for several islands in the Caribbean.

There were significant innovations in military architecture during this period, most notably the construction of forts whose plans originated with the Marquis de Sébastien Le Prestre Vauban (1632–1707), the great French designer of forts who was the chief military engineer for Louis XIV (Hanson 1972; Vauban 1968). The concept of using bastions to catch an enemy in the crossfire originated with Vauban, who ultimately was even more in demand for his siegecraft than for his fort designs. He was at his best in designing equipment with which to attack forts. Many of the more permanent forts in the colonies were inspired by his novel designs, including Louisbourg, Crown Point, Fort Ticonderoga, Fort Edward, Fort William Henry, Fort Ponchartrain, and Fort Massac. However, it should be remembered that there were many designers of forts during this period, not just Vauban.

From the very beginning, the French built expensive, sophisticated fortifications, whereas British defenses typically relied upon small forts, little more than walled enclosures. While the latter may have been effective against Indian attacks, they could not withstand French artillery. It was not until the English built Fort Edward and Fort William Henry, both in 1755, that they finally mastered fort construction.

Most French and Indian War forts were designed for the ongoing warfare between the British and the French, and this had prompted many small communities to construct forts for mutual defense. Nevertheless there were many other sites that were essentially fortified trading posts, promoting prosperity through trade. Fort Michilimackinac, Fort St. Joseph, and many others were primarily interested in commerce to ensure alliances with local native populations, and their fortifications were essential to protecting the fur trade.

Research Projects

A great many archaeological projects have been conducted at French and Indian War sites, and the examples that follow are organized geographically, running from Michigan (Fort Michilimackinac and Fort St. Joseph) to Pennsylvania (Fort Necessity and Fort Ligonier), West Virginia and Virginia, New England (forts in Maine, Massachusetts, and Vermont), and, finally, New York. This list is by no means exhaustive, and other period forts—such as the 1756 Fort Dobbs in North Carolina—extended into nearby colonies (Babits 2010).

Fort Michilimackinac

Fort Michilimackinac on the Straits of Mackinaw in Michigan has been a park since 1857, and it has made archaeology an integral part of its interpretive programs since 1959. As of 2009, this represents 50 years of excavations at the fort, making Fort Michilimackinac the site of the longest continuous excavations in North America. This work is universally respected because of the fort's active publications program that has widely disseminated the results to both professional and popular audiences. Projects led by Lyle Stone, Donald Heldman, Roger Grange, and most recently by Lynn Evans have intensively explored this settlement, which was first built and occupied by the French in 1715 to protect the fur trade and then later occupied by the British.

Archaeological digs every summer have exposed the remains of many buildings, the palisade, post molds, hearths, wells, and countless artifacts (Stone 1974; Evans 2003; Grange 1987). Some of the buildings excavated at Fort Michilimackinac include the powder magazine, a provision store, a blockhouse, blacksmith shops, houses within the Southeast and South Southeast Rows, and the Solomon-Levy Trading House. The quality and variety of material culture at this distant frontier outpost are exceptional, representing multiple cultures and reflecting the extensive trade with Native Americans. Artifacts stored in the collections at Fort Michilimackinac include glass trade beads, crucifixes, finger rings, bone combs, harpoons, fishhooks, rosary beads, gaming pieces, and just about every other type of eighteenth-century material culture (Evans 2003). The collections and exhibits at Fort Michilimackinac are an excellent source of information about early trade in the Great Lakes.

Fort St. Joseph

A more recent, ongoing investigation in this same area is the project being conducted at Fort St. Joseph on the lower St. Joseph River in southwestern Michigan. Research since 1998 by Western Michigan University archaeologists, directed by Michael Nassaney, has successfully located this 1691

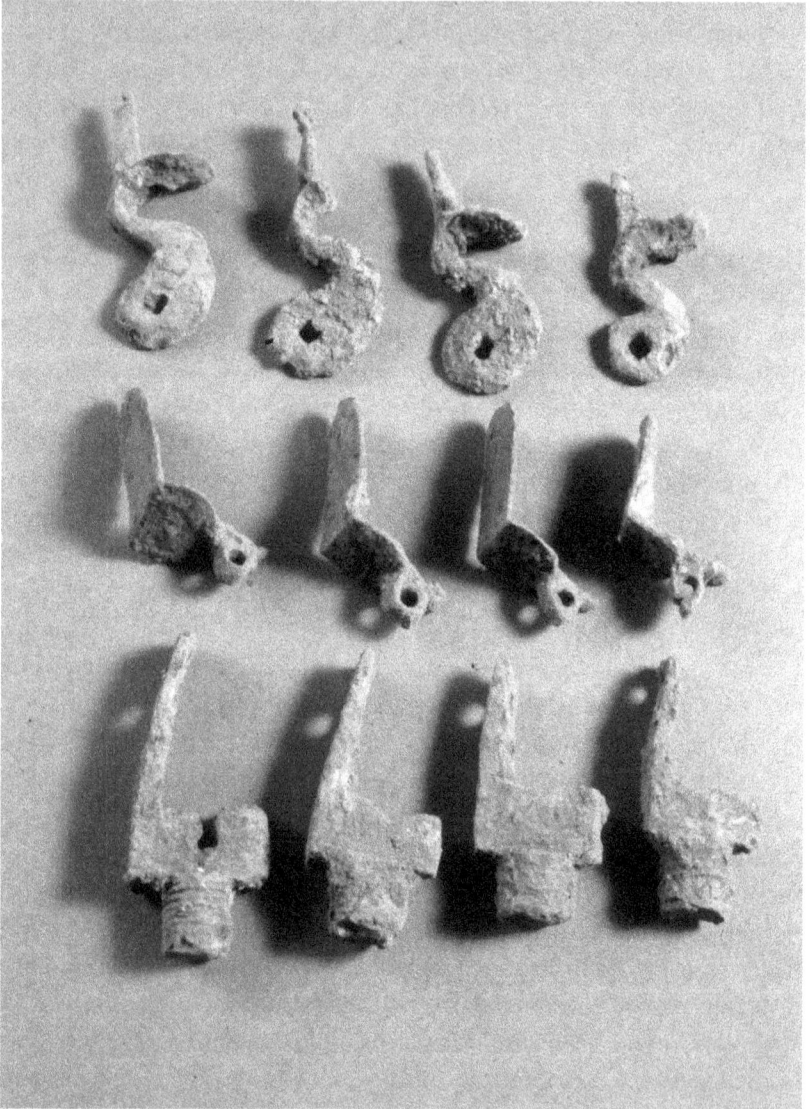

Figure 4.1. These flintlock gun cocks, frizzens, and breech plugs were recovered from a cache of more than 100 gun parts at Fort St. Joseph. They likely represent an activity area associated with one of the gunsmiths that occupied the fort during the first half of the eighteenth century. One of the services provided to natives at this center of commercial and military activity was the repair of guns, many of which were employed in the Chickasaw Wars and other military engagements involving the residents and allies of Fort St. Joseph. (Photo courtesy of Michael Nassaney.)

mission, garrison, and trading post, which played an important role in the eighteenth-century French fur trade in the western Great Lakes (Nassaney, Cremin, and Lynch 2002–4; Nassaney et al. 2003).

Farmers began plowing up relics here in the late nineteenth century, but because portions of the site are now below water, the high water table necessitated that Nassaney's team create a well-point system to extract groundwater. Several geophysical techniques have also been employed to locate features, including electrical resistivity, electromagnetic conductivity, ground-penetrating radar, and magnetometry. These techniques have proven successful in locating several building features, fireplaces, a rich cache of musket hardware (frizzens, cocks, and more) (figure 4.1), large quantities of butchered animal bones, and a variety of French and British artifacts from the late seventeenth and eighteenth centuries. French daily life at Fort St. Joseph was greatly influenced by the presence of Indians nearby (the Potowatami), and many Indian artifacts were found here, as well as numerous copper-alloy tinkling cones. Fort St. Joseph was clearly a major outpost in the western Great Lakes region, and it appears to share many similarities with Fort Ouiatanon along the Wabash River in western Indiana, excavated by Michigan State University in the 1970s (Martin 1986; Noble 1979; Tordorff 1979).

Fort Necessity

One of the most famous of the smaller forts early in the French and Indian War is Fort Necessity in the Ohio country of western Pennsylvania. It was here that a very inexperienced George Washington and about 400 Virginia Militia and British regulars from South Carolina faced a force of about 700 French soldiers and Indians from Fort Duquesne on July 3, 1754. This was part of the 10-year contest between France and Britain for control of the vast inland area along the Ohio and Allegheny rivers. After constructing a small stockade with entrenchments around it and then fighting for most of a day, Washington surrendered to the French commander, Captain Louis Coulon de Villiers, and was allowed to march his men back to Virginia.

Although the French burned the fort, Washington's only defeat left behind an archaeological site that would be of interest to several generations of researchers. Excavations there in 1901 and 1931 failed to determine the correct shape of the stockade—researchers believed it to have been three-sided or four-sided—and it took meticulous excavations by

Figure 4.2. The reconstructed circular log stockade at Fort Necessity in western Pennsylvania. The reconstructed fort occupies the site of the original fort, and the vertical posts are in exactly the same location as the original stockade posts.

J. C. Harrington in 1952–53 to establish that Washington's troops had built a 53-ft-diameter circular stockade (figure 4.2); however, archaeology has failed to locate the small log storehouse that history placed inside the stockade.

The bases of many of the posts, some of them charred, were still well preserved below the water table (Harrington 1957, 1976). Ironically, the greatest difficulty faced by Harrington was the considerable disturbance caused by the 1932 excavation and reconstruction. Earlier excavators, determined to prove that there were historical misconceptions about the location and shape of the stockade, had caused much damage to the site. While Fort Necessity was never a carefully designed fort and was intended to be just an enclosure for protecting supplies, its association with George Washington—his first test as a military commander—make this one of the most significant battle sites of the French and Indian War.

Fort Ligonier

While perhaps not as imposing as Fort Ticonderoga, one of the finest examples of a fort excavation that aided reconstruction was that of Jacob Grimm at the site of Fort Ligonier in western Pennsylvania. The fort had been constructed as part of the ongoing struggles between the British and French for control of the land west of the Allegheny Mountains, and Fort Ligonier was a supply base during the campaign against Fort Duquesne. Fort Ligonier successfully repelled a French attack on October 12, 1758, and then a later Indian attack on June 21, 1763, during Pontiac's Rebellion. Built in 1758, the fort was constructed with an inner fort of logs, nearly 200 ft on a side and with bastions in each corner, surrounded by an outer fort of log entrenchments.

Allowed to fall into ruin after 1766, the remains of Fort Ligonier saw a small excavation in 1947 and reconstruction in 1954, but it was Grimm's excavations between 1960 and 1965 that located many key features inside the fort. Grimm excavated 610 5-ft squares, and he exposed magazines that led to much more accurate interpretation of the fort. For its day, Grimm's site report (Grimm 1970) presented one of the best discussions of excavated military features, and his analysis of Fort Ligonier's artifacts—still housed at the fort today—was exceptionally thorough, permitting comparisons with the artifacts that have been found at other British forts of the period. Every military camp had slightly different sources of supply, and archaeology can demonstrate regional and chronological differences in provisioning.

Fort Ashby, Fort Edwards, and Fort Vause

Stephen McBride of McBride Preservation Services and Kim McBride of the Kentucky Archaeological Survey have been excavating three French and Indian War forts, the sites of Forts Ashby and Edwards in West Virginia and Fort Vause in Virginia. (See Malakoff 2009: 36 for the route of these forts.) These were small forts with corner bastions and stockade walls, and the construction of Fort Ashby was ordered by George Washington in 1755 as part of his larger chain of forts meant to protect Virginia settlers against the French to the west.

Soon afterward, Fort Edwards, a privately built fort that Washington subsequently included within his Virginia defenses, was built on land owned by Joseph Edwards, a settler. However, both forts were short lived. At Fort Edwards, Stephen McBride directed excavations in 2001 and 2004 "that uncovered more than 50 features associated with the fort, including several stockade walls, a bastion, and what appears to be the foundation of Joseph Edwards' home" (Malakoff 2009: 37).

Small-scale excavations at Fort Vause in Virginia have revealed some of the walls and three bastions made of earth, rather than logs. A principal interpretation made by the McBrides is that the fortifications built by civilians were quite different from (more irregular than) those built by professional soldiers. The artifacts at the settler forts are also more diverse and more likely to be domestic in origin.

Fort Pemaquid and Forts on the Coast of Maine

Few regions of the United States possess as many fort sites as the coast of Maine, and a great many of these sites have been excavated. These span both the seventeenth and eighteenth centuries, but chief among these are the forts of Pemaquid, Maine, where both Helen Camp and Robert Bradley conducted excavations intermittently over many years (Bradley 1981; Bradley and Camp 1994). The continuing struggles between French and British in the region ensured that the fortifications at Pemaquid would be destroyed repeatedly, beginning in 1676 and continuing until 1759. As each new fortification was destroyed by the French, this left an enormously complicated but fascinating set of ruins that continues to entice Maine archaeologists to dig there.

The Line of Forts: Fort Pelham and Fort Shirley

Ephraim Williams Jr. commanded a row of small log forts built west of the Connecticut River in Massachusetts between 1744 and 1763 to protect English settlers from attacks by the French and their Indian allies. These were constructed across the northern Berkshires, and the largest fort, Fort Massachusetts, was built in 1745 in North Adams, near the western end of the line. The next fort to the east was Fort Pelham, also built in 1745 and located in the town of Rowe; and then Fort Shirley, built in 1744, was another five miles to the east, in the town of Heath. These were essentially palisaded blockhouses, with garrisons of only 40–50 men.

Fort Massachusetts has never been excavated, but more than 75 percent of Fort Pelham was dug by Daniel Ingersoll and field schools from the University of Massachusetts, Amherst, in 1971 and 1972. Later, a smaller proportion of Fort Shirley was excavated by Michael Coe and volunteers from Yale University in the summer of 1974 (Coe 2006). At the site of Fort Shirley, Coe excavated less than a third of the blockhouse site (which had measured 60 ft on a side), along with drainage ditches, barracks areas, and one of the fort's wood-lined wells. At Fort Pelham, Ingersoll's much larger excavation exposed the remains of a large barracks structure for which

Figure 4.3. Excavating the western corner of Fort Dummer in Brattleboro, Vermont.

nail densities were plotted in an effort to determine the configuration of the building. In studying both of the forts, Coe has noted that almost none of the material culture at these frontier forts was locally made, and he refers to the flood of consumer items into the forts as the "Consumer Revolution on the Massachusetts Frontier" (Coe 2006: 136).

Fort Dummer

A short distance to the north, one of the least-well-known (and most difficult to dig) forts from this time period is Fort Dummer, the first permanent English settlement in Vermont. Built in 1724 and located just south of Brattleboro, Fort Dummer was abandoned in 1760, and its remains now lie underneath the waters of the Connecticut River. Still, because of maintenance performed on the nearby dam that had first submerged the site in 1905, the river was lowered for just one week in 1976, and a team of volunteers went to work removing overburden (Harrington 1978). With amazing luck, given how little time was available, the team found walls from the westernmost corner of Fort Dummer (figure 4.3). The sand and mud were wet-screened, great quantities of period artifacts were found, and then the river rose again. In the space of only a week, this was easily one of the most productive fort excavations ever undertaken.

Fort St. Frederic

Traveling a short distance to the northwest, Fort St. Frederic was built by the French at the southern end of Lake Champlain so that France could trade with Indians in upstate New York and so that French farmers could move into the Champlain Valley. Occupied between 1731 and 1759, and consisting of a citadel, chapel and ovens, this fort was crucial to the early French occupation of the region, but they were later forced to blow up the fort and retreat in 1759 because of an approaching British army led by General Jeffrey Amherst. New York State later acquired the site and briefly allowed excavations by Roland Robbins in 1968, at which time he exposed the walls of the Light Infantry Redoubt as well as military dumps (Kravic 1971; Starbuck 1999: 168). This site has seen only modest archaeology since that time, chiefly for compliance purposes.

Fort Ticonderoga

A few miles to the south of Fort St. Frederic is another French fort, the site of Fort Ticonderoga, constructed at the orders of the governor of Canada in 1755. Originally called Fort Carillon, the fort was positioned so as to overlook both Lake Champlain and the outlet of Lake George, thus controlling travel between Canada and the American colonies. This is an excellent example of a Vauban-style fort, constructed with two demilunes and with bastions extending out from its four corners (figure 4.4).

Throughout its history "Fort Ti" was the site of numerous attacks, and modern marketing proclaims that "three times the fort was attacked and held, and three times it was attacked and fell." Allowed to fall into ruins, the site was purchased by William Ferris Pell in 1820, and the eventual restoration project was led by Stephen Pell, who opened Fort Ticonderoga to the public in 1909 with President Taft in attendance. At that time some digging was used to find the bases of the original stone walls, and the fort was rebuilt on top of early foundations. Most of the surrounding area, occupied by extensive military encampments during both the French and Indian War and the American Revolution, has never seen formal archaeological excavations, although great research potential exists, especially for early French sites. Impressively large collections of period artifacts, maps, and historical documents are in storage at the Thompson-Pell Research Center at the fort.

Figure 4.4. The reconstructed main entrance of Fort Ticonderoga in northern New York State.

No archaeology was conducted at Fort Ticonderoga until 1957 when part of the French village was dug by J. Duncan Campbell and members of the Pell family (Campbell 1958). The French village had been constructed for the men who were building the fort, and Campbell's dig helped to locate the foundations of buildings lying between the fort and the edge of Lake Champlain. These buildings included a blacksmith shop, a bakehouse, storehouses, a wine shop, a trader's store, and dwellings for civilians.

More recently, an extensive excavation was conducted in 2001 into the terre-plein at Fort Ticonderoga by Elise Manning-Sterling and Bruce Sterling of Hartgen Archeological Associates. This dig was followed by a 2005 excavation into the Magasin du Roi in preparation for the construction of the new Mars Education Center, and this involved digging the entire eastern side of the fort, from the northeast bastion down the east flank and to the southeast bastion. The recent work at Fort Ticonderoga has revealed well-preserved eighteenth-century features just about everywhere the archaeologists have dug (Manning-Sterling 2004: 21–22).

Figure 4.5. The interior of Fort Niagara State Historic Site.

Fort Niagara

Many years of excavations have been conducted at Fort Niagara State Historic Site, initially by Stuart Scott and Patricia Scott of the State University of New York at Buffalo (Scott 1998; Scott and Scott 1990; Scott et al.
1991), and more recently by Elizabeth Peña and Susan Maguire of Buffalo
State (Peña 2006). Located on the Niagara River near Buffalo, New York,
Fort Niagara was constructed by the French in 1726 to control the portage
around Niagara Falls, and in the early 1750s it was used as a primary base
within the French line of forts along Lake Erie and the Ohio River. It left
French hands in 1759 after it was besieged by a British army, and it subsequently remained in British hands throughout the Revolutionary War
and up until 1796.

Archaeological work by the Scotts commenced in 1979, and they successfully identified many architectural features throughout the fort. At
least 250 buildings are known to have been erected here over a 300-year
period (figure 4.5), and summer field schools, combined with an on-site
laboratory, are ensuring that Fort Niagara is one of the best-known sites
of both the French and Indian War and the American Revolution, with
extensive artifact collections housed at the fort.

Fort Edward and Rogers Island

Arguably the bravest of the forces that served during the French and Indian War were the rangers, and the most famous of these were Rogers' Rangers, named after Major Robert Rogers of New Hampshire. Every New England provincial regiment had its own ranging company, but Rogers was different in that he trained other officers in how to conduct woods' warfare. Significantly, he was the first to actively promote an "American" style of fighting (Todish 2002; Zaboly 2004). The rangers were among the greatest woods fighters of all time, and they fought using tactics adopted from the Indians. These rugged frontiersmen fought the French and Indians throughout the forests of northern New York, New England, and Canada, and they were the most celebrated Indian fighters of the mid-eighteenth century.

Throughout the French and Indian War, Rogers and his rangers circulated in that part of New York in-between the British forts in Lake George and Fort Edward, and the French forts in Crown Point and Ticonderoga. Occasionally forays extended even farther, and when Rogers attacked and burned the Abenaki village of Saint Francis (now Odanak) in Quebec in 1759, it was in retribution for the raids made by the Saint Francis Indians upon the British settlements to the south. Known among Native Americans as "the white Devil," Rogers put St. Francis to the torch, and it is claimed that he killed Abenaki women and children during that raid. Revenge killings went back and forth throughout the French and Indian War, and the English, French, and Native Americans all believed they had the moral high ground.

History has presented Rogers as always on the move, but he did have one long-term base camp, and that was Rogers Island in the Hudson River in upstate New York, about forty miles north of Albany. Together with Fort Edward on the east bank of the river, this complex was the largest British base of the French and Indian War with some 15,000–16,000 British soldiers, provincial soldiers and rangers from the colonies of New Hampshire, Massachusetts, Rhode Island, Connecticut, New Jersey, and New York. This enormous encampment seasonally became the third largest city in America as soldiers and supplies arrived, as men drilled, and as they prepared to travel north to attack French and Indian positions. Rogers' Rangers occupied Rogers Island between 1757 and 1759, and it was there that Rogers wrote the "Rules of Ranging" in 1757, his guide to

Figure 4.6. The excavation of a two-sided barracks fireplace on Rogers Island in Fort Edward, New York.

Figure 4.7. The excavation of a hut site on Rogers Island in Fort Edward, New York. Three rows of nails were all that survived from the floor of the hut. The presence of a floor and the solidly constructed fireplace on the right suggest either an officer's hut or a structure that was substantial enough to be occupied through the winter.

irregular forest warfare. That distinction has caused Rogers Island to be declared the "Birthplace of the U.S. Army Rangers."

While British Regulars lived within massive barracks buildings on Rogers Island (figure 4.6), each perhaps as much as 300 ft long, the rangers built log huts for shelter (figure 4.7). In excavations that have been ongoing since 1991, we have excavated a number of these, as well as tent sites and British barracks (Starbuck 1996, 1997a, 2004a). Rogers Island was never built upon during the years after the war, so the sites of barracks buildings, huts, tents, storehouses, kilns, and hospitals are amazingly well preserved.

These military structures were intended to last for no more than a few years, the duration of a campaign, and probably the most distinctive building was the smallpox hospital at the southern end of Rogers Island. We discovered and excavated this and its associated dump in 1994, revealing the outline of an earthfast building surrounded by a palisade wall (Starbuck 1997b; 2004a: 68–77). This was the first smallpox hospital ever professionally dug in North America, fortunately containing no tissue

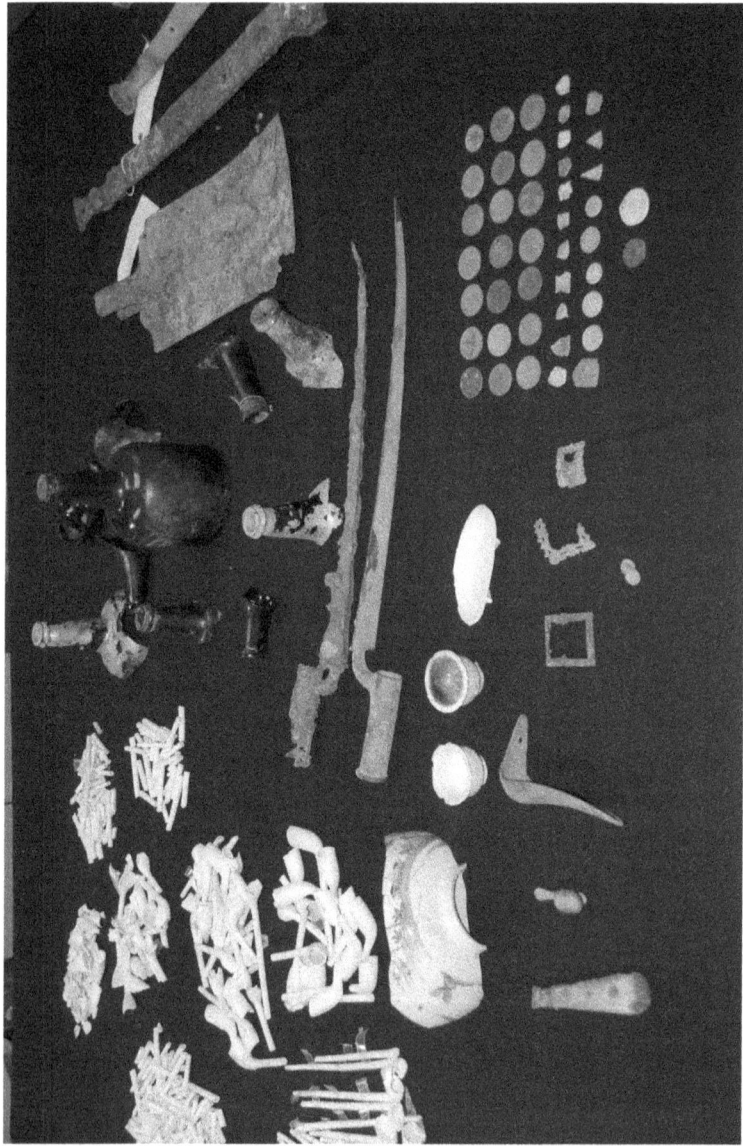

Figure 4.8. Examples of artifacts discovered inside the sutling house in Fort Edward, New York, which was a source for many of the supplies sold to the British army in the 1750s. The musket parts and bayonets are from British "Brown Bess" muskets, the coins are chiefly British half-pence and Spanish cobs and milled coins, and the ceramics are tin-glazed earthenware and white salt-glazed stoneware.

samples that could have transmitted the smallpox virus to modern-day diggers.

Rogers Island now survives as one of the most pristine and celebrated sites of the French and Indian War, in no small part due to the mystique that surrounds Rogers' Rangers. The rangers were the quintessential Americans: feisty, independent, and widely considered to have been the most likely to be sent to the whipping post for disobeying orders because they were not inclined to obey British officers. Wide-ranging excavations over many years have made this one of the most thoroughly researched sites of the French and Indian War. Unfortunately, most of these artifacts are no longer available for study in Fort Edward; some are housed at Fort Ticonderoga, and the remainder are in private hands.

Artifacts recovered at this and other French and Indian War sites include a variety of armaments (musket parts, musket balls, grapeshot and canister shot, gunflints, and innumerable bits of melted lead from the casting of musket balls), earth-moving and forest-clearing tools (axes, wedges, brush knives, spades, shovels, and hoes), food remains, and items of personal adornment that sometimes help us connect on a more intimate level with soldiers and officers. Buttons, buckles, cufflinks, pins, and clothing hooks and eyes all suggest personal preferences that we can appreciate and admire. Health care and maintenance are visible in the form of medicine bottles, bandage pins, and medicine/ointment jars, and everywhere at French and Indian War camps there are tobacco pipes and wine bottles, evidence for some of the "vices" or leisure activities shared by soldiers everywhere.

This last point is exemplified at the recent excavation of the remains of a 1750s sutling (merchant) house on the Hudson River in Fort Edward. Here archaeologists have discovered great numbers of tobacco pipes, wine bottles, buttons, and drinking glasses that suggest the presence of a tavern (figure 4.8). Just as important was the discovery of over 70 British and Spanish coins, suggesting that a great deal of commerce was going on between the army and the sutlers. Only at a sutling camp were soldiers and officers able to purchase those things not supplied as regular military issue (Starbuck 2007, 2008, 2010). Fortunately, the large collection of artifacts from the sutling house is available for study through the auspices of the Rogers Island Visitors Center in Fort Edward.

Final Thoughts

While this is a fairly small sampling of some of the British and French forts that clashed in the mid-1700s, each fort was typically at the center of an enclave that represented the beginnings of European settlement in the eastern United States. Many forts stimulated and protected local trade with Native Americans, and many gave way to towns and cities in the years that followed. As towns grew up around them, forts were no longer needed and were torn down, and building materials were often salvaged and recycled by early settlers. While none of these forts is fully intact today, it has been possible for archaeology to uncover and to permit reasonably accurate reconstructions of many of them. Early forts and battlefields are thus very much still with us, and they continue as a very exciting part of the American experience.

Case Study: Fort William Henry on Lake George

One of the few stories of the French and Indian War that still resonates today is based on events at Fort William Henry, a small log fort located at the southern end of Lake George in upstate New York. Its notoriety stems from the so-called massacre that occurred there in August 1757, immortalized by James Fenimore Cooper in his novel, *The Last of the Mohicans* (Cooper 1980 [1826]). This was the northernmost British fort to be erected after the Battle of Lake George in 1755, and it was one of the first carefully designed British forts in the American colonies, a bastioned fort in the French style. William Eyre was the engineer who designed the fort in the fall of that year on the orders of William Johnson, and it was a relatively safe outpost for nearly two years. But undeniably, forts are remembered less for their strategic positioning or innovative designs and more for the battles and deaths that occurred there. The story of Fort William Henry is unequaled by events at any contemporary fort because the great siege of the fort by a force of about 10,000 French and Indians ended with the brutal killing of unarmed British soldiers, after which hundreds of British prisoners were taken to Canada and held for ransom.

The construction of Fort William Henry began late in 1755, and its location was dangerous from the outset because of its northern position on land claimed by the French. The log fort contained four barracks buildings, storehouses, a hospital, a magazine, and sheds, all of which surrounded a central parade ground. A moat and 30-ft-thick walls of earth and logs surrounded the whole. The garrison of about 2,300 was a mixture of British soldiers and colonials, and the commanding officer was Colonel George Monro, a career officer, a Scotsman, who held out for six days before surrendering to the French commander, Louis-Joseph de Montcalm-Gozon, Marquis de Saint-Véran.

While the French promised an armed escort that would deliver their prisoners to safety, this seemingly made little difference when some of Montcalm's Indian allies (Abenakis and representatives of about two dozen other Canadian tribes) attacked the retreating prisoners on the Old Military Road, which ran south for fifteen miles to the nearest British fort at Fort Edward. No firm figures have ever been obtained for the number of killed and captured, but while early chroniclers claimed that as many as 1,500 of the British had been killed, more recent reassessments have placed the number of dead at fewer than 200 (Steele 1990: 143).

After the surrender, the French removed any supplies they could use, burned the fort, and returned north to Fort Carillon (Ticonderoga) from whence they had come. In one of the supreme ironies of this campaign, after the siege some of the Indians allied with Montcalm dug into the graves of the military cemetery that lay outside the fort, scalping the dead and stealing blankets and clothing. Many of those who lay in the British cemetery had died from highly contagious diseases, and the smallpox that was transmitted to the Indians at this time resulted in much death along the trails running north to Canada. For those who actually made it home, the smallpox they carried with them soon destroyed whole villages in Canada.

For the next 200 years, the ruins of Fort William Henry were largely neglected, although the publication of Cooper's novel in 1826 kept the events of 1757 well known in historical and literary circles. Movies served much the same purpose in the twentieth century, and the 1936 version with Randolph Scott, and the 1992 remake with Daniel Day-Lewis, are certainly the best-known adaptations. After all, the adventures of Hawkeye, Uncas, and Chingachgook make for a rousing good story!

The surface of the fort site was marked with a few paths for visitors, a gazebo was added much later (it appears in photographs from the early 1900s), and the top of the fort's well has appeared above the surface of the ground down to the present day. However, it was not until the 1950s that the site was purchased by businessmen who wanted to develop the fort as a tourist destination, and archaeology then became an aid to reconstruction. A nonprofessional archaeologist, Stanley Gifford, was hired to oversee the work, and between late 1952 and 1954, the northwest bastion of the fort was completely excavated, along with part of the parade ground and an edge of the fort's cemetery (Gifford 1955; Starbuck 1990b, 1993b). Fragments of mortar bombs, cannonballs, buckshot, axes, pewter spoons, knives, tobacco pipes, canteens, and much, much more were found within the charred ruins, and this collection is still housed at the fort today.

One of the more unusual artifacts was a human scalp with black hair, stuck to the side of a mortar shell that had never exploded. Had this been lobbed by the French into the fort, and had it careened off the skull of some unfortunate soldier or officer? There also were Native American artifacts in the ruins, spanning 8,000 years and demonstrating that Indians had lived there long before the soldiers arrived. Many thousands of visitors watched the 1950s archaeology, and then new walls were quickly thrown up, guided by the archaeological finds as well as by the original engineers' drawings, which showed how the fort had been laid out.

Very little was published about Gifford's work, except in newspapers, but the reconstructed fort became a staple of tourism in the village of Lake George. From 40,000 to 60,000 tourists a year passed through the front gate and viewed the artifacts recovered from the site *The Last of the Mohicans* had made famous. Another 40 years went by, and the owners of the fort site decided that it was time for further archaeology. I was contacted, and aided by students and volunteers, our excavations at the fort were conducted from 1997 until 2000 (Starbuck 2002b, 2007). Our work included digging throughout the parade ground (figure 4.9), in the fort's well, in an extensive dump outside the east wall of the fort, in the moat, and around the perimeter of the cemetery. Everywhere the first few feet had been disturbed by the reconstruction project in the 1950s, but below that we encountered burned soil and entered the world of the 1750s soldiers.

After Gifford's excavation, a key question had been whether the "new" buildings of the reconstruction had been placed accurately on the original foundations. Modern visitors invariably wanted to know the answer, and in the absence of a final excavation report, there was no clear sense of the reconstructed fort's authenticity. The work of the 1990s helped to locate some of Gifford's undocumented trenches, and in the process we discovered that the West Barracks—which had been completely

Figure 4.9. An excavation trench at the northeast corner of the parade ground at Fort William Henry.

reconstructed—had been rebuilt about 8 ft to the west of the actual foundation. From an archaeological perspective, this was, of course, quite wonderful because it meant undisturbed archaeological deposits.

We were able to dig deeply inside the strata of the barracks, recording the burned layers of soil from the time of the fort's destruction, and discovering the outlines of rooms on the cellar floor (figure 4.10). We found the base of a barracks fireplace, staining from beams and large posts, and everywhere there were artifacts. These included sherds of tin-glazed earthenware and white salt-glazed stoneware from plates and cups, musket balls and gunflints, sewing paraphernalia, fragments of wine glasses and other drinking glasses, and even fragments of exploded mortar bombs, probably marking the fort's destruction by the French.

The dumps that lay just east of the fort, in the direction of Lake George, were rich and deep, extensive enough to confirm a large garrison over a lengthy period of time. The soldiers had thrown their garbage down a steep slope, and we dug an enormous "step trench" perpendicular to the outer wall of the fort, 12 ft deep, revealing great quantities of butchered animal bones, pottery sherds, fragments of wine bottles, tobacco pipes, buttons and even a Jew's harp, one of the few musical instruments to be discovered at the fort.

Much of what we found was no doubt quite representative of a frontier fort in the 1750s, a mix of trash from meals, clothing, and armaments, accompanied by just a few artifacts that suggest leisure activities (the tobacco pipes and the Jew's harp). The one context we excavated that was a bit out of the ordinary was the fort's stone-lined well, originally dug in 1756 by Rogers' Rangers and located at the north end of the parade ground. Gifford's team had conducted a partial excavation inside the well in the 1950s, giving up when they hit the water table.

Not to be deterred by the possible danger, in 1997 we erected a hoist over the top of the well and inserted a culvert inside to prevent the walls from collapsing. I became the digger in the well and slowly worked my way down through about 11 ft of post-1955 "tourist artifacts" and then through the debris that had fallen in over the long years the well stood open. Finally, over 25 ft below the modern ground surface, I arrived at a 1750s stratum in which soldiers had dropped musket balls, gunflints, tobacco pipes, and bits of lead into the well, lined at the bottom with 3-in-thick planks.

Figure 4.10. The excavation into the foundation of the West Barracks at Fort William Henry. Most of the cellar had been left intact during the restoration of the fort in the 1950s, and the barracks contained a wealth of information about British soldiers in the 1750s.

The well did not contain bodies or horrific evidence of the massacre. Instead, French and Indian War soldiers would probably have been startled, and perhaps amused, to learn that thousands of tourists had deposited coins, sun glasses, plastic toys and chewing gum on top of the soldiers' humble trash, all sparked by present-day curiosity about the lives of eighteenth-century soldiers (Starbuck 2001).

Today Fort William Henry stands again as a reconstructed, commercial tourist attraction, but that does not take away from the excitement that most visitors feel when standing atop one of the most historic settings in eighteenth-century America. Without archaeology, Gifford's and ours, what would they be able to experience? Tales of Hawk-eye and Colonel Monro are all very fine, but the past needs to be three-dimensional and documented by archaeology to be truly appreciated.

Visitors need to look up at the log walls and imagine the French lobbing mortar bombs over the ramparts, they need to see the surrounding terrain to imagine the French siege trenches drawing closer and closer, and they need to walk inside the parade ground to realize that a small, cramped space actually housed a thousand or more soldiers while the British army was under attack. Archaeology is essential for this experience to become "real" for a modern-day visitor, and this experience is further heightened by today's military reenactors, who add even more realism and immediacy to the experience (Starbuck 2008b).

5

The American Revolution

Fewer than 20 years separated the French and Indian War from the opening events of the American Revolution (1775–83), and the two wars were interlinked in many ways, not the least of which was in the identities of those doing the fighting. It is often noted that many of the ranking officers at the time of the Revolution had served together during the previous war, and their experience raised them to leadership positions. It is true that the expenses incurred during the French and Indian War led to the severe taxation that helped to precipitate the Revolution, but Americans in the 1770s, while still thoroughly British, were an increasingly self-confident and independent people, capable of choosing their own destiny.

Although forts had been integral to defensive strategies of the French and Indian War, the significance of long-term fortifications had declined, and fast-moving Revolutionary War forces left behind a host of encampments, winter cantonment sites, and battlefields. Frontier forts had lost much of their efficacy, and the residents of small towns no longer needed a fort to protect themselves from Indian attack.

During the Revolution the tactics of the American and British sides differed significantly. In general British forces were well disciplined and held their ground in open fields. In contrast, the American preference was to *skirmish* with the British and to avoid direct confrontation. Typically that meant the Americans shot at the British *from cover* and picked away at the British a few soldiers at a time.

There also were several changes in material culture that had occurred in between the time of the French and Indian War and the American Revolution. Creamware had now been widely adopted, whereas tin-glazed earthenware and buff-bodied, slip-decorated earthenware were fading away. But even more distinctive was the introduction of numbered regimental buttons and insignia, a most helpful guide to determining the physical placement of regiments within encampments and in battle settings. There also appears to have been a decline in the frequency of tobacco pipes (and tobacco) at Revolutionary War sites, perhaps reflecting changing tastes, but more likely revealing a difficulty in transporting goods from southern, tobacco-growing colonies to the North because of the several British-controlled areas between.

Research Projects

Forts

His Majesty's Fort at Crown Point, the largest British fort in North America, was constructed and occupied between the two wars but did not really see service during either war. It was commenced in 1759 by General Jeffrey Amherst, and about 8,000 men were involved in its construction. The huge barracks buildings there were made to look like two-story Georgian mansions, strung together in groups of four (figure 5.1).

Unfortunately, a major fire in 1773 caused all of the barracks at Crown Point to burn, and then the powder magazine blew up. Totally abandoned after 1777, it was later acquired by New York State, which has periodically sponsored excavations there prior to building stabilization and below-ground disturbances (Feister 1984a, 1984b; Fisher 1995). Some of this work has proven extremely useful in demonstrating class differences between officers and enlisted men, and Lois Feister (Huey) has determined that the officers' barracks had tile floors and brick fireplaces, whereas the enlisted men's barracks had brick floors and limestone fireplaces (Feister 1984a). Today the site and the artifacts are under the management of the New York State Office of Parks, Recreation and Historic Preservation.

Running past Crown Point is the waterway that General John Burgoyne used to transport his army of British and German soldiers south from Canada in the summer of 1777. Burgoyne's several-month campaign created dozens of camp sites and battlegrounds along the hundreds of miles connected by Lake Champlain, Lake George, and the Hudson River. Elsewhere I have termed this route the "Great Warpath" (Starbuck 1999a), and a few miles south of Crown Point is the narrow isthmus on Lake Champlain that was flanked on opposing shores by Fort Ticonderoga (New York) and Mount Independence (Vermont). It was there that pa-

Figure 5.1. The barracks buildings inside His Majesty's Fort at Crown Point. The officers' barracks is in the left foreground and the soldiers' barracks in the right rear.

triot forces tried, unsuccessfully, to block Burgoyne's invasion. (See "Case Study: Mount Independence on Lake Champlain," page 60.)

A second major fort that spanned the two wars was Fort Stanwix in Rome, New York. Fort Stanwix was built by the British in 1758 to protect the Oneida Carrying Place, the trail that connects the Mohawk River with Wood Creek. Later, in 1776, it was ordered rebuilt by the Continental Congress and was occupied by American forces after that date. The fort was besieged by the British under Colonel Barry St. Leger for three weeks in 1777 during the same campaign in which Burgoyne sought to split off New York from the New England colonies. American forces at Fort Stanwix successfully withstood the siege, and the fort was finally abandoned in 1781. A small dig was conducted there by J. Duncan Campbell in 1965, and later, thanks to a downtown urban renewal project, the 12 blocks that contained the remains of Fort Stanwix were excavated by Dick Ping Hsu for the National Park Service.

Hsu's investigations began in 1970, and he excavated a variety of structures over the next two summers. The fort was then completely reconstructed (figure 5.2), and today artifact collections continue to be stored at the fort (Hanson and Hsu 1975). About 33 percent of Fort Stanwix was

Figure 5.2. The reconstructed fort at Fort Stanwix National Monument in Rome, New York, one of the last forts to be reconstructed anywhere in the United States.

dug, and archaeology was key to the reconstruction. However, this type of project was a bit of an anachronism, and Stanwix became the last fort anywhere in the United States to be rebuilt by the National Park Service. This was largely because it was finally coming to be recognized that such reconstructions are inherently inaccurate because historical records and drawings are often wrong and archaeological features may be interpreted in multiple ways. In the past it was almost universally believed that the public needed to see forts as three-dimensional recreations, essentially "monuments to the past," but each reconstruction is but a reflection of the best interpretations *at that moment in time*, a "best guess" scenario. What are the owners and managers of reconstructed forts supposed to do when they discover that key elements of their reconstructions are just plain wrong?

Several other Revolutionary War forts have seen extensive excavations, one of the best of these projects being at Fort Montgomery, located on the lower Hudson River just above New York City. Construction of Fort Montgomery began in March 1776, and combined with Fort Clinton, its purpose was to block British shipping on the Hudson. The buildings that are historically documented within the fort include two barracks for soldiers, an officers' barracks, storehouse, powder magazine, bake house, guard house, necessary, and battery of six 32-pounder cannons. The fort came to an end after events on October 6, 1777, when a British fleet bombarded the fort and the garrison surrendered.

While some archaeology was attempted at Fort Montgomery as early as 1916, it was not until the period between 1967 and 1971 that Jack Mead excavated numerous buildings and features in anticipation of the reconstruction of the fort. Today Fort Montgomery State Historic Site is managed by New York State's Office of Parks, Recreation and Historic Preservation, and together with staff from the New York State Museum, they have conducted excellent research on the previously assembled artifact collection (Fisher 2004). Among their findings there is evidence for differences between officers and soldiers who lived at the fort:

> Artifacts, such as the large ceramic collection, indicate food preparation and consumption varied among the social groups present at the fort. Creamware, for example, was associated with officers' quarters and represented meals of dry meat served on flatware and consumed with knives and forks. In contract, the soldiers' primary ceramics were hollowwares of slip decorated yellowware. They were used to hold liquid based foods that were consumed with the aid of spoons or with bare hands. (Fisher 2004: 155)

Different foods, different methods of food preparation, and different wares all help to distinguish between the different social worlds occupied by officers and soldiers at Fort Montgomery.

Other excavated Revolutionary War forts include Fort Laurens, located about 60 miles south of Cleveland, Ohio (Gramly 1978). Richard Michael Gramly excavated most of Fort Laurens in 1972 and 1973 and used dietary remains to show that officers ate much more fresh meat than did the enlisted men. His findings were also helpful in demonstrating that certain tools were to be found only in the refuse of the enlisted men, whereas tea sets/tea drinking was only to be found among the officers (Harral 1993: 8–9). And, somewhat to the south and east, Stephen and Kim McBride are excavating the well-known site of Fort Donnally as part of the Frontier Forts Project. Fort Donnally was a stockaded Revolutionary War frontier fort in the Greenbrier Valley of West Virginia, best known because it was attacked by a large force of Wyandots and Mingoes on May 29, 1778. One corner of Fort Donnally was actually the house of Andrew Donnally, and the stockade walls of the fort abutted Donnally's house (McBride 2006).

Battlefields

The Battle of Saratoga is usually referred to as one of the 20 or 25 most important battles in world history, and events that transpired there have caused it to be termed the "Turning Point of the Revolution" because it prompted France to join the war on the American side. The two battles fought there in 1777 between about 17,000 American soldiers and fewer than 7,000 British and German soldiers (at Freeman's Farm on September 19 and Bemis Heights on October 7) halted General John Burgoyne's invasion from Canada and ended the British northern campaign of 1777. It was the first great American victory of the war, and British and American redoubts, other fortifications, hospitals, and camp sites left behind an enormous complex of archaeological sites, now linked together by a nine-mile-long tour road within Saratoga National Historical Park. The battle areas are maintained by the National Park Service, and all artifacts from many years of excavations are housed within the park.

Sporadic archaeological digs began at the Saratoga Battlefield as early as the 1930s, and compliance work in the 1950s and 1960s by John Cotter and Edward Larrabee was followed by an extensive mapping project conducted by the State University of New York at Albany between 1972 and 1975. In what would become the first thorough surface mapping of any American battlefield, Dean Snow and his students (Snow 1977, 1981) produced 38 base maps of the battlefield, mostly at a scale of 1:1500. Excavations into redoubts and other features were used to increase the accuracy of the mapping.

Later excavations at the Saratoga Battlefield were conducted by David Starbuck and Rensselaer Polytechnic Institute into the sites of the American headquarters, the British lines (the "British Old Woods"), the Taylor House (where Brigadier General Simon Fraser died after the battle on Bemis Heights), and nearby at the Philip Schuyler House (which had been burned by the British shortly before the first Battle of Saratoga). Relatively few battle-related artifacts were found—chiefly musket balls—and most discoveries pertained to the local farms that existed both before and after the battles (Starbuck 1988; 1999b: chap. 2). The paucity of military artifacts was not unexpected, but Saratoga has not yet been subjected to a thorough metal-detector survey which might be able to increase our knowledge of movements over the surface of the battlefield.

A short distance away lies the Bennington Battlefield, only about eight miles west of Bennington, Vermont. It was there where American militia under Brigadier General John Stark resoundingly defeated a force of German soldiers, Tories, and Indians who had been sent out from General Burgoyne's army to collect supplies and cattle. The German soldiers were chiefly Brunswick Dragoons who served under Lieutenant Colonel Friedrich Baum, and while well disciplined, they were no match for American skirmishers and for superior American numbers. An enormous number of historical documents have been gathered to analyze movements of soldiers throughout the battle, and Philip Lord and the New York State Museum conducted archaeology there, recovering very few period artifacts (Lord 1989).

While Saratoga and Bennington have experienced traditional excavation, historical research and surface mapping, the Monmouth Battlefield in Freehold, New Jersey (now Monmouth Battlefield State Park), has witnessed much more innovative types of research (Sivilich and Stone n.d.). The Battle of Monmouth saw 4,000 Americans attack a British army on June 28, 1778, in what has become known as the longest battle of the American Revolution (including an artillery duel that lasted between two and a half and three hours). British general Sir Henry Clinton's army of 20,000 had left Philadelphia and was marching across New Jersey toward New York City with General George Washington and the American Continental army in pursuit. Washington's men had just spent the winter at Valley Forge, and they caught up to Clinton's rear guard in the town of Monmouth Courthouse, New Jersey, where they then attacked the rear of the British column. Six thousand British soldiers turned to fight the Americans, and at the end of the day, the Continental army still held the field and the British army continued moving north.

In order to better understand the details of the battle, Daniel Sivilich and Ralph Philips formed the Battlefield Restoration and Archaeological Volunteer Organization (BRAVO) and began to use metal detectors to locate musket balls and other artifacts from the Battle of Monmouth. Because the British "Brown Bess" musket used a ball that is .69 caliber, and the French Charleville musket used by the Americans had a ball of .63 or .64 caliber, this has enabled BRAVO to identify each ball on the battlefield according to the side that fired it. (Any ball larger in diameter than .66 in

Figure 5.3. Daniel Sivilich (*center*) is demonstrating how BRAVO enters data from the total station (*left*) into a laptop computer in order to generate artifact distribution maps of the Monmouth Battlefield.

typically was used in the Brown Bess musket.) Because some balls were flattened and their diameters could not be measured, each musket ball was also weighed to determine its caliber. Once it was determined who had fired each ball, Sivilich and his colleagues could then begin to extrapolate troop positions and movements throughout the Battle of Monmouth.

As musket balls and other artifacts are located in the field, Sivilich then bags, tags, and flags each artifact. A total station (transit) is used to precisely locate each artifact (figure 5.3), and positioning is entered into a CAD-generated map of the Monmouth Battlefield. By revealing where shells and clusters of grapeshot and canister shot had landed, the archaeologists can then show where American cannons and British how-itzers had been positioned and their targets. Many of the musket balls are found to have tooth marks, and Sivilich argues that "soldiers would chew on cool lead musket balls to promote salivation" (personal communication, January 9, 2009), whereas other soldiers may have bit down on these during battlefield surgery just as their limbs were being sawn off. Other balls have tooth indentations, the shape of which suggest they had been chewed upon by pigs.

Monmouth is witnessing some of the most sophisticated battlefield archaeology in the United States today. Thanks to very innovative ways of looking at musket balls, Sivilich has made the convincing argument that the Battle of Monmouth was an American victory, cementing Washington's position as leader of the Continental army (Sivilich 1996). While it cannot be demonstrated archaeologically, Sivilich likes to point out that soldiers of the Revolutionary War feared bayonets far more than they feared musket fire, which was relatively inaccurate, and the British army loved to terrorize Americans with bayonet charges (Sivilich, personal communication, October 21, 2005).

Encampments/Cantonments

Many encampments and winter cantonments dating to the American Revolution have been sampled by professional archaeologists, including Valley Forge (Pennsylvania), Morristown (New Jersey), Pluckemin (New Jersey), the New Windsor Cantonment (New York), Camp Redding (Connecticut), and Mount Independence (Vermont). None of the others is as famous as Valley Forge, near Philadelphia, where General George Washington and about 12,000 men of the Continental army camped under hardship conditions from December 1777 to June 1778. Within an area of about 2,000 acres, the army initially lived in tents, and later they constructed more than 1,000 log huts (14 × 16 ft each) (figure 5.4). Hundreds

Figure 5.4. Reconstructed log huts at Valley Forge National Historical Park in Pennsylvania, site of the winter cantonment for the Continental Army in 1777–78.

of American soldiers died there, and in the process they left behind an enormous archaeological site of defensive earthworks and redoubts, log huts and offal pits, all with ample evidence for construction techniques, subsistence, and provisioning.

The Museum Applied Science Center for Archaeology (MASCA) at the University of Pennsylvania conducted a great deal of remote sensing at Valley Forge National Historical Park to locate hut sites, and a considerable amount of excavation has occurred there as well (Parrington 1979, 1979–80; Parrington, Schenck, and Thibau 1984). John Cotter taught his first historical archaeology class there at Wayne's Woods (the Pennsylvania Brigade) beginning in 1960, and other excavations have been conducted in the Outer Line Brigades and Conway's Brigade. Teams from Temple University under David Orr and Carin Bloom are currently conducting excavations at the Washington Chapel site. Sizable areas within Valley Forge have never been plowed, so there may be a lot that is still intact (David Orr, personal communication, January 9, 2009). It has often been observed that, while no great battle occurred there, Valley Forge is a powerful symbol of the suffering that Americans were willing to accept in order to obtain their independence, and it is an archaeological site that helps to demonstrate what soldiers were willing to endure as they waited to fight.

Morristown is located about 35 miles west of New York City, and it is managed as Morristown National Historical Park by the National Park Service. Composed of many separate sites, Morristown consists of Washington's Headquarters (1779–80), Fort Nonsense (1777), the Jockey Hollow Encampment area (1779–80), the Pennsylvania Brigade Encampment site (1779–80), and the New Jersey Brigade Encampment site (1779–80). It is the high integrity of these many sites that make this one of the very best parks for interpreting the Continental army during the Revolutionary War.

As many as 11,000 soldiers were camped at Morristown, in orderly rows of winter huts, and General George Washington established his headquarters there in 1779 in the home of Theodosia Ford. Excavations at the sites of many of the huts began in the 1930s, later followed by the more careful excavations of John Cotter, Edward Rutsch, and others (Rutsch and Peters 1977). Some testing of Fort Nonsense was conducted by Edward Rutsch in 1971 (Rutsch and Skinner 1972), and there have been comprehensive studies of the extensive artifact collections housed at the park (Synenki and Charles 1983).

Numerous hut sites were reconstructed in Morristown beginning in the 1930s, but unfortunately these reconstructions destroyed original archaeological features. Still, much is known about hut placement at Morristown. For example, each regiment occupied 24 huts, and these were arranged in 2, 3, or 4 rows, with 12 men to a hut. These huts typically measured 14 × 16 ft, the same as at Valley Forge. Taken as a whole, Morristown is enormous, it has a great many well-preserved archaeological sites, and its remains have the potential to tell the story of the suffering endured by the Continental army as they encamped there in the winter of 1779–80.

Pluckemin was the winter site of General Henry Knox's 1778–79 Continental Artillery Cantonment, and it was occupied by companies of Continental artillery, armorers, artificers, and others, all for a relatively brief period. Beginning in 1979, John Seidel excavated at Pluckemin within the sites of enlisted men's and officers' barracks, artificers' quarters, and an armorer's shop (Seidel 1983, 1987). Seidel was especially focused on using material culture to demonstrate status differentiation, but he used artifact groups (Kitchen Group, Architecture Group, and Activity Group as defined by South [1977]) to determine the status of the soldiers who lived in each line of huts. In doing so, Seidel concluded that the Academy Line had been occupied by enlisted men, the Northeast Line by officers, the Southeast Line by artificers, and the North Line by enlisted men. Seidel's use of archaeology at Pluckemin is one of the most successful studies of social ranking that has been conducted at any military site.

Very thorough research at a Revolutionary War cantonment has also been conducted by Charles Fisher at the winter cantonment for the Continental army at New Windsor (near Newburgh), New York. Between November 1782 and September 1783, about 7,000 men along with 500 women and children constructed and then lived in about 600 log dwellings at New Windsor. This was a year after the Americans had defeated the British at Yorktown, Virginia, and conditions were somewhat better than at previous Continental army cantonments. Construction details of the huts were much more standardized than at earlier cantonments, with each hut measuring 18 × 35 ft, divided into two rooms, and with eight men per room. A fireplace was constructed at each gable end, and each hut had two doors. To reinforce status distinctions between officers and enlisted men, the officers' huts had 8-ft-tall ceilings and 6-ft-tall door openings, while the enlisted men's huts had 7-ft-tall ceilings and 5-ft-tall door openings.

Today the New Windsor Cantonment is managed by the New York State Bureau of Historic Sites, and Charles Fisher was able to devote years of research to studying status distinctions at New Windsor (Fisher 1983, 1984–85, 1986a, 1986b, 1987). The high degree of regimentation, the opportunities to examine collections from officers' dumps and to compare these to enlisted men's dumps, and the chance to determine whether only officers' huts used window glass were all variables studied by Fisher at New Windsor.

Camp Redding in Redding, Connecticut, was the location of the Continental army winter cantonment in 1778–79 (December to April), placing it one year after the winter encampment at Valley Forge and one year before the winter encampment at Morristown. Some of the huts and refuse pits at Camp Redding were excavated by David Poirier in 1973 and 1974 (Poirier 1976). More recently, Daniel Cruson has excavated the remains of enlisted men's huts and an officer's quarters at Camp Redding (Cruson and von Jena 2002; Cruson 2001), using archaeological remains to show differences (regional variations) in hut construction between New Hampshire regiments and Canadian regiments.

Case Study: Mount Independence on Lake Champlain

While the most famous battlefield sites of the American Revolution are surely at Saratoga and Yorktown, and the best-known cantonment is surely that at Valley Forge, there is a little-known hilltop on the east shore of Lake Champlain at present-day Orwell, Vermont, that is easily one of the most intact archaeological sites of the war (Wolkomir 1998). Prior to 1776, Mount Independence (the "Mount") was a forested peninsula in western Vermont, jutting out into Lake Champlain at the narrowest isthmus on the lake. The Mount was positioned just a quarter-mile across the water from the older fortifications at Ticonderoga in New York, and in combination the two forts had the potential to stop any British invasions from Canada by catching all enemies in a crossfire as they sailed down the lake.

It was General Philip Schuyler who gave the orders in early 1776 to fortify the hilltop and make it the major northern fortification for the

American army. Soon after, the chief engineer, Jeduthan Baldwin, aided by Polish engineer Thaddeus Kosciusko, used the American northern army to clear the woods and erect fortifications in the summer of 1776 (Baldwin 1906). As American soldiers gathered there from New York, New Jersey, New Hampshire, Connecticut, and Massachusetts, the Declaration of Independence was read to them on July 28, 1776, and then a log fort, blockhouses, barracks, batteries, hospitals, and hundreds of lookout posts were quickly erected in anticipation of a British assault.

Three brigades (12 regiments) of American soldiers lived atop the Mount into the fall of that year, in rows of huts and tents, and a small number lived on through the hard winter. A fourth brigade was positioned across the water at Fort Ticonderoga, and the combined army numbered about 12,000 men when at peak strength. Baldwin constructed a floating bridge across Lake Champlain at this point, anchored by 27 log caissons, so that soldiers could walk back and forth over the water between the two forts. The floating bridge was created by pushing log cribbing out onto the ice in the winter, and the cribs sank to the lake bottom when the ice melted in the spring of 1777. Just north of the bridge, a massive chain was stretched from shore to shore across the lake to block any British ships that might try to force their way through.

The defenses at Mount Independence were first tested in October 1776, when Sir Guy Carleton, governor general of Canada, and 8,000 soldiers sailed down Lake Champlain and approached the fortifications at the Mount and Ticonderoga. With a curious mixture of luck and good planning, the Americans did not need to fight on that occasion because the British took one look at the heavily armed American forts, turned around, and returned to Canada. Most of the Americans left the site before the onset of bad weather, and surviving journals record how quite a few of those who remained at the Mount froze to death during the winter.

Few soldiers returned in the spring of 1777, and the Americans were not well prepared that summer when a second British army, that of General John Burgoyne, returned and quickly swept an American force of only 3,000–4,000 men from the two sides of the lake. In the face of an enormous British fleet, with perhaps 500 Indian allies, the Americans and their leader, General Arthur St. Clair, fled from the two forts on July 5–6, 1777, rather than face seasoned British Regulars. As the British strategy unfolded, they first entered Fort Ticonderoga, and then their advance guard charged across the floating bridge to Mount Independence as the

Americans fled from their attackers. A small American rear guard, left behind to blow up the bridge, was discovered "dead drunk by a cask of Madeira [wine]" (Anburey 1789: 323–325). This was not the finest moment for patriot forces during the American Revolution. With the Americans gone, and the Mount now occupied by British forces, the new occupants of Mount Independence drew a map, the 1777 Wintersmith map, which is one of the finest maps to have survived for any military encampment of the war.

While this was a demoralizing American defeat, the implications for modern archaeology are obvious: A great many buildings were erected in a rural setting, they were occupied for about a year, and then the buildings were burned by the British in the fall of 1777 and never built upon again. Mount Independence became an enormous time capsule, covering 300 acres, with foundations, earthworks, and artifact scatters lying everywhere under the trees. And under the waters of Lake Champlain are the remains of the floating bridge, the log caissons that the plank deck was anchored onto. The Lake Champlain Maritime Museum has prepared extensive underwater documentation of the log caissons (McLaughlin 2000; Starbuck 1999b: chap. 8), and all across the bottom of Lake Champlain, paralleling the bridge, are the remains of cannonballs, shot, spades, and even muskets dropped by soldiers crossing the lake while on the bridge.

Generations of Vermonters picked up artifacts from the surface of the Mount, rarely needing to dig because so little soil had built up atop the shallow bedrock. A herd of cattle "mowed the grass," a couple of signboards greeted visitors, and several marked trails wound through the woods on the site. It was all very idyllic and certainly very pristine. Visitors who wanted to see major exhibits or reconstructed buildings were disappointed and quickly left. After all, if they crossed the lake, they could see a reconstructed Fort Ticonderoga, rather than just foundations at Mount Independence. But for those who wanted to see original fabric, this really became the ultimate contrast in how to present the past: The footprints from nearly all of the buildings are still clearly visible at the Mount, whereas many elements at Ticonderoga are a twentieth-century interpretation of the eighteenth century.

The Vermont Division for Historic Preservation manages and interprets the ruins atop Mount Independence, and they hired me in the summers of 1989, 1990, and 1992 to direct excavations and to map the surface of the Mount. During that time, my field crews identified over

50 Revolutionary War structures based on the presence of low earth and stone mounds, identifiable by the stones from collapsed chimneys and fireplaces (Starbuck 1993; Starbuck and Murphy 1994; Howe 1991). The low earth mounds stood out so conspicuously against the forest floor that it was relatively easy to identify the remains of cultural sites but harder to determine their extent and function(s). After all, most of the hut sites had been occupied for just several months, there was no mortar between the stones, and all of the wood had rotted away.

The very ephemeral nature of front-line military camps such as this left so few traces behind that nothing less than a full-scale excavation could establish building perimeters, fireplaces, door or window locations, or the extent of associated dumps. We found armaments, axes, buttons, clothing hooks, spades, and more. We also learned very quickly that the presence/absence of glass tablewares, window glass, and personal adornments are all very helpful in determining the status of the occupants of each site. Officers clearly enjoyed the "extras" that came with their rank and means, and their affluence was reflected in the material culture that we were finding in some of the cabin sites, including wine glass fragments and cuff links.

The most common structures we discovered and sampled atop Mount Independence were small, three-sided lookout posts, and there were easily 100 or more of these. But of the many archaeological features we found, several were noteworthy examples of very specialized activity areas. Perhaps the most interesting of these was the General Hospital, erected in the months leading up to the British attack in July 1777. As a "general" hospital, every type of medical case could be dealt with there, but smallpox patients would be shipped elsewhere because of the danger of contagion. The American leadership knew that there would be significant casualties once Burgoyne's army arrived from Canada, so this hospital was primarily intended to handle battlefield injuries. Historical drawings show a building that measured 250 ft long by 25 ft wide, with a wing still being added at one end that would have turned the hospital into an L-shaped structure.

Because the Americans fled their posts in such an impromptu fashion that July, we really did not know whether the General Hospital had been used very much, but we certainly wanted to find out. Our excavations (and those of a Vermont game warden in the 1950s) successfully located the stone rubble from four large fireplaces inside the hospital foundation, as well as fragments of glass medicine bottles, medicine cups of white salt-glazed stoneware, ointment jars, knives, and hundreds of fragments of wine bottles (Starbuck 1990a, 1997b). The artifact scatter was quite thin, and the hospital appears to have seen little actual use. We know from history that the hospital was abandoned just as the British army approached, so the few patients inside would have been ones with illnesses rather than battle injuries. A surgeons' mate, James Thacher, described removing all medical supplies and all but four of the sick from the hospital just before the British attacked (Thacher 1862).

About 46 meters to the north of the hospital, we excavated a large disposal pit full of butchering debris, consisting of the lower legs from 17 cows that had been consumed either in the hospital or in adjacent huts (figure 5.5). This was tangible evidence that the soldiers had brought livestock with them, a chance to have fresh meat in addition to the usual fare of salted beef and pork. Ironically, this was not the only large-scale butchering evidence we discovered because no more than 100 meters to the northeast we found an equally large scatter of cow legs that still lay exposed on the surface of the ground after 213 years! (Because of the exposed bedrock, every last artifact on the Mount is no deeper than 6 in or so.)

Among the most ubiquitous structures on Mount Independence were the many small tents, log cabins, and plank houses that soldiers and officers occupied. Few of these were drawn on any engineer's map or etched into any powderhorn, yet the small dwellings were laid out in long rows over much of the Mount, especially where the land was relatively flat.

We chiefly focused our activities in the area where the 2nd Brigade had been encamped, and these were soldiers from New Hampshire, Massachusetts, and New York. Historical documents identified the origins of these soldiers, but so did the regimental buttons that we often found during the cabin excavations: buttons from the American Fifth, Twelfth, Twenty-second, and Twenty-fifth Regiments, and the British Fortieth and Forty-seventh Regiments. So many wine bottles were found that we sometimes joked about how drinking was the "favorite leisure activity" of the soldiers, but there also were butchered bones from cows, pigs, sheep, and fish. Historical records note that the men were told *not* to keep taking the boats out to go fishing because the officers never had the boats when they needed them for military duties.

The cabins also contained scatters of nails, buckles, and pottery sherds of creamware, white salt-glazed stoneware, delft, and unrefined stoneware.

Figure 5.5. A refuse pit full of butchered cow legs atop Mount Independence on Lake Champlain, evidence for the consumption of fresh meat at the site.

As we dug the cabin sites, there is no question we were "connecting" with the ordinary men who fought for the American side during the Revolution. After all, a *battlefield* is a moment in time, and collectors have heavily looted most battlefields. But a long-term *encampment* is where it is possible to appreciate the very "human" qualities of the soldiers—all of the little things that they ate, wore, and valued—or, in the words of James Deetz, the "small things forgotten" (1977).

Interestingly enough, there were two categories of artifacts that were missing from the Mount. First, coins were almost nonexistent. We found one Spanish silver cob and nothing else; a possible interpretation for this is that the soldiers here had little to buy, no cash economy, and they lived a very isolated existence. Second, after three years of excavations, we found only a few tobacco pipe fragments. This, too, may suggest a very Spartan existence, and it raises the question of whether supply lines could not reach Virginia and other tobacco-growing colonies. Scholars love to point out that life was difficult at Valley Forge, but there may have been winter cantonments, far from supply lines, where life was even grimmer.

The remains of the log fort on top of Mount Independence have never been dug, but there were several blockhouses atop the Mount, and we

Figure 5.6. The excavation of the foundation of one of the blockhouses at the site of Mount Independence. At the time of this photograph, the central fireplace had not yet been exposed.

excavated the foundation of one of these in 1989 (Starbuck and Murphy 1994: 120). Shaped like a minifort, with thick log walls that overlooked the southeast approach to the Mount, this impressive structure measured 30 ft on each side (figure 5.6). It had probably been two stories in height and would have contained one or more cannons, pointed downhill toward approaching enemy forces. In the center of the foundation was the base of a very intact fireplace that opened on two sides, but there was very little trash inside. The presence of architectural artifacts—large nails and spikes that had been used in the construction of the blockhouse—but few personal or food artifacts would suggest that the soldiers lived elsewhere and manned the blockhouse only when on sentry duty.

One of the more curious finds at Mount Independence came during the 1992 season, when we decided to expose all of the features within a battery at the southeastern corner of the Mount. Our efforts were rewarded with the discovery that a series of five huts had been erected against a natural stone outcrop, probably occupied by those who manned cannons along the front edge of the battery. The most interesting of these huts contained the flattened fragments from two kidney-shaped canteens, two lead netsinkers (each about the size of a musket ball), a wrought-iron hook for hanging a pot over a fire, and the usual assortment of nails, wine bottles, butchered bones, musket balls, and pottery sherds.

None of these artifacts appeared out of the ordinary, and it was not until we processed the artifacts in the laboratory that we found the only *personalized* artifact ever discovered on Mount Independence: a nearly complete wine bottle that had the name and date "James Hill 1777" scratched onto two sides. Personal inscriptions are rare at military camps, where so much is "standard issue," so this provided a direct link to one of the soldiers who may have lived inside this hut. The bottle is on display today inside the Mount Independence Visitors' Center museum, which was built after we completed our excavations. The distinctively shaped museum building has the shape of an upside-down bateau, and the inscribed wine bottle is the most provocative of the many Revolutionary War artifacts on display there. The Vermont Division for Historic Preservation stores or displays all of the artifacts recovered from Mount Independence excavations at the museum.

In the years since my own work was completed at Mount Independence, the state of Vermont has sponsored additional surveys and limited

Figure 5.7. The "talking heads" of soldiers inside the Mount Independence Visitors' Center.

excavations at the Mount. They have created new walking trails and sign-boards. And they have even erected an elaborate walkway running along-side the General Hospital foundation, providing a view of the foundation stones. The most popular exhibit, though, is a set of "talking heads" inside the Visitors' Center, portraying soldiers who are reciting some of the his-tory of the Mount (figure 5.7). The talking heads are fascinating, but per-haps the exhibit designers should have modeled these after the archaeolo-gists who dug at the Mount: The talking heads of a group of archaeologists would have been a thrill. And the "head" of the chief archaeologist could have told visitors:

> This is the way to present a Revolutionary War site. You do not re-build "monuments to the past." Rather, you use nature trails, tasteful signboards, and lots and lots of original foundations and artifacts to show your audience what has actually survived from the past. Mount Independence is the real deal.

6

The American Civil War

The American Civil War (1861–65) is an enormous topic, heavily researched, intensively published upon (e.g., Foote 1974; Catton 1965; McPherson 1988), and deeply personal to the millions who are descended from combatants. More than 600,000 Union and Confederate soldiers were killed in the war; in fact, after just one battle, the Battle of Gettysburg, more than 51,000 soldiers were dead, wounded, captured, or missing (see figure 6.1). Adding to this immense popular interest are the thousands of reenactors who recreate the battles and the camp life of those who fought in the Civil War. Extensive war correspondence, early photography, vast numbers of letters sent home from the field, and enormous collections of Civil War weapons, clothing, and accouterments tell a story so rich that archaeology may seem a bit redundant. What additional stories can possibly be told?

If the names of commanders and the strategies employed at Civil War battlefields are best known from historical research, then perhaps the greatest strength of Civil War archaeology is to delineate the "cultural landscape" within an encampment, showing, for example, how tens of thousands of men dealt with their comrades and how they constructed their cookhouses, huts, and latrines. More than 10,000 Civil War battle sites have been identified (Nash 2004: 25), but unfortunately there is very little money with which to acquire and protect additional sites, and battlefields are constantly being lost to development and relic hunters.

This problem does not receive as much attention with earlier American battlefield sites, partially because there are so many sites from the Civil War, but also because so many mid-nineteenth-century sites are located near large population centers where commercial development has already occupied and altered all available land. An additional problem is that the Civil War is so intensely personal for many Americans that just about

Figure 6.1. The Little Round Top at the Gettysburg Battlefield.

everyone wants to collect and own "a piece of history" in the form of military buttons, bayonets, or minie balls. The Civil War was fought among our own people and in our own back yards, and the temptation to collect is enormous.

Research Projects

Until fairly recently, there was no such thing as "Civil War archaeology," although relic collectors have long employed their metal detectors around the edges of state- and federally owned battlefields. The inevitable result was that very few Civil War sites were untouched, and some professional archaeologists may have considered these sites to be too recent or picked-over, or just not capable of adding significantly to the voluminous historical literature about the Civil War.

Fortunately, that picture has now radically changed. Every annual meeting of the Society for Historical Archaeology since at least 1990 has held one or more symposia devoted to excavations at Civil War sites. Most of the work being reported involves cultural resource management surveys, often incorporating the use of remote sensing using ground-penetrating radar, electrical resistivity, and magnetometers. Every single effort is ultimately a preservation project, with the work focusing on the unprotected perimeters of battlefields and with archaeologists rushing to document sites that are slated for development. Almost daily, newspapers trumpet this destruction, with a typical headline reading, "Historians Battle Wal-Mart over Key Civil War Site." (This headline actually appeared on January 5, 2009.) On the other hand, there also have been projects that have achieved enormous positive media coverage, such as the discovery of the long-lost Confederate submarine *H. L. Hunley*, as I describe in the Case Study below.

Many archaeological contract reports and assessments have been written for Civil War battlefield sites, but when compared to the archaeology that has been conducted on earlier wars, the literature on Civil War archaeology is rather limited. Still, this is rapidly changing, and some excellent results are contained within Geier and Winter (1994), Geier and Potter (2000), and Geier, Orr, and Reeves (2006). Recent excavations at the City Point, Virginia, headquarters for Ulysses S. Grant during the Petersburg campaign (Orr 2006); Camp Nelson, Kentucky (McBride and McBride 2006); the site of the Battle of Antietam in Maryland (Sterling and Slaughter 2000; Potter and Owsley 2000); the Manassas Battlefield in northern Virginia (Galke 2000; Seibert and Parsons 2000); and Andersonville Prison in Georgia (Prentice and Prentice 2000) all provide exciting insights into the Civil War. Most important, these projects suggest that Civil War archaeology has successfully moved beyond the rich documentary record.

Andersonville Prison is easily the most infamous of the Civil War prisons, and to be able to study life inside a Civil War military prison is a tremendous research opportunity for archaeologists. Still, it is a sobering task to deal with the remains of a "prison camp in which, by August 1864, 33,000 Union POWs were crowded into a space of 25 acres—32 square feet per man—without shade in a deep South summer" (Rintels 1996: xi). Nearly 13,000 prisoners died at Andersonville, more than 100 deaths each day, and the mortality rate here was about 29 percent.

Andersonville National Historic Site in Andersonville, Georgia, has seen archaeology since the early 1970s, and at that time excavations were used to locate stockade lines and stockade corners, revealing important aspects of the footprint of the prison site. More recently, investigations by the National Park Service's Southeast Archeological Center from 1987 to 1990 exposed more stockade lines, part of the north wall of the prison, and numerous well-preserved posts. The artifacts that were recovered can only hint at the prisoners' lives, but Andersonville has tremendous potential for revealing just how wretched the conditions really were for Civil War prisoners. An additional benefit of the research in 1990 was that, quite unexpectedly, they discovered "a failed prisoner escape tunnel . . . the only archaeological data collected to date regarding prisoner escape tunnel construction at Andersonville. . . . The tunnel was approximately 20 inches high, just big enough for a man to crawl through" (Prentice and Prentice 2000: 185–86).

Another ongoing archaeological project at a Civil War prison is the work being conducted by David Bush (Heidelberg College) at Johnson's Island Civil War Military Prison in Ottawa County, Ohio, where over 10,000 Southern officers were confined between April 1862 and September 1865. Successive summer field schools have exposed features such as the prison stockade, portions of two prison blocks, a well, a powder magazine, a ditch that had been dug down to bedrock to keep prisoners from escaping, and more. But perhaps the most interesting features to be dug are some of the latrines on the island. The latrines were used for very short periods of time, and their contents give unparalleled insights into the medical treatment of Southern prisoners of war while demonstrating that the prisoners had access to a much wider range of material culture than might be expected inside a military prison.

The years of research at Johnson's Island are now accompanied by the very first excavations at Camp Lawton, Georgia, on the grounds of Magnolia Springs State Park. Camp Lawton was the 40-acre prison that supplemented Andersonville in the fall of 1864, and 700 men died here in just six weeks. The stockade of this recently discovered site is being excavated by Sue Moore (Georgia Southern University), and the camp's long period of obscurity has led to excellent preservation of archaeological remains.

These prison projects help to demonstrate that the last-minute salvage of earthworks and staging areas is no longer the primary objective of much of Civil War archaeology. The very nature of research has broadened, and archaeology is now used to demonstrate that the Civil War had an impact upon almost every aspect of nineteenth-century life. Archaeology has the potential to study the war's effect upon slavery, economics, industry, and material culture. Civil War archaeology has now begun to examine camp life, troop movements, the popularity of pork over beef, the variation in button types, the availability of alcohol, the configuration of earthworks and encampments, and myriad other topics.

Case Study: The Confederate Submarine *H. L. Hunley*

Eight skeletons, eight uniforms and eight pairs of shoes. Thanks to archaeology, this assemblage brings closure to one of the most inspirational stories of the Civil War. Nothing can quite compare with the near-legendary mystery of eight brave Confederate sailors who challenged a well-armed Union warship, the USS *Housatonic*, and then disappeared. On the night of February 17, 1864, the sailors quietly guided their submarine, the *H. L. Hunley*, four miles out from Charleston Harbor, rammed a torpedo into the hull of the enemy sloop, pulled away, signaled to shore that they had been successful, and then vanished, seemingly forever.

Many false guesses were made as to the design and appearance of the submarine (figure 6.2), but it was not until 1995 that modern-day researchers, funded by famed author Clive Cussler, succeeded in discovering the remains of the *Hunley* and its crew, and another five years before archaeologists successfully raised the *Hunley* to the surface (figure 6.3). Then began the long process of conservation that continues today under the auspices of the Friends of the *Hunley* (Hicks and Kropf 2002; Huntington 2005).

Figure 6.2. An early replica of the Confederate submarine *H. L. Hunley* outside the Charleston Museum. This recreation was based largely on conjecture and demonstrates quite effectively the need for archaeology to bring accuracy to the past.

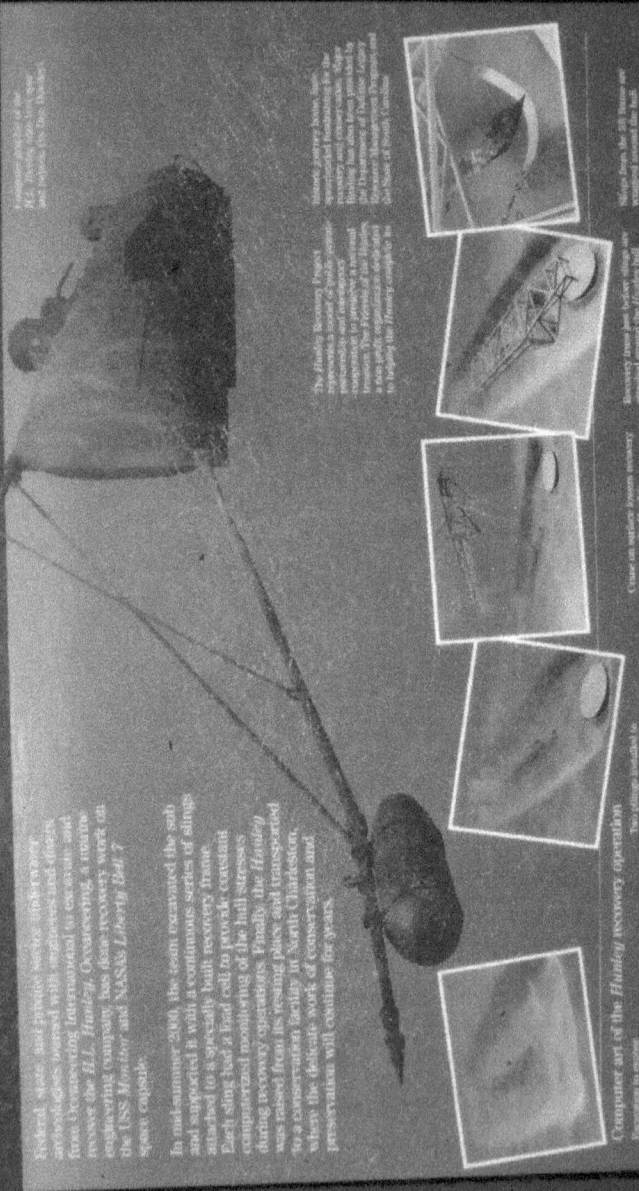
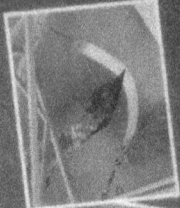
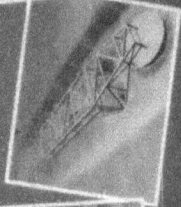

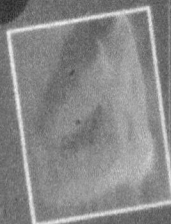

Figure 6.3. A recent signboard at Charleston Harbor describing steps in the Hunley Recovery Project.

The *Hunley* was an amazingly small craft, and in its day it was described as a "diving torpedo-boat." Today it is remembered as the first submarine in history to sink an enemy warship. The *Hunley* was built in Mobile, Alabama, in the spring of 1863 before being sent to Charleston, South Carolina, where it was to prey upon the Union ships that were bombarding and blockading Charleston's harbor. Powered by a hand-cranked propeller, the 40-ft-long *Hunley* had two conning towers, and each was topped with a tiny hatchway that allowed the crew to squeeze inside. Once they were seated on a wooden bench that ran along the port side, in a space that measured just 4 ft tall and 3.5 ft wide, the submarine descended by virtue of ballast tanks in the bow and stern. The tanks were flooded to make the *Hunley* sink and then pumped out so that it could rise. A bellows, drawing air through "snorkle tubes," exchanged air with the surface. The hull itself was made from cast-iron plates of various sizes that were riveted together end to end.

While simple in design and quite ingeniously built, the *Hunley* had twice proven deadly to its own crew, drowning a total of 13 men on previous test dives, including its namesake, New Orleans lawyer and planter Horace Lawton Hunley. After the second failure, rescuers were forced to saw the arms off the blackened, bloated corpses in order to remove them from the submarine. Still, the South continued to experiment with submarines because they needed to relieve the Union blockade that threatened to paralyze all Confederate shipping. A submarine that sank Union ships would terrify the North even as it gave encouragement to the Southern cause. Several other submarines were constructed, by both sides, throughout the course of the Civil War (Oeland 2002).

On February 17, the leader of the *Hunley*'s crew was Lieutenant George Dixon, and he was accompanied by seven Confederate volunteers who left Battery Marshall on Sullivan's Island at about 7:00 p.m. They slowly propelled their way by turning a zigzag iron crankshaft that ran through the center of the cramped vessel. The captain, Dixon, used a compass as he sat at the helm, guiding his crew to their target. The sailors had mounted a torpedo containing 90 lbs of black powder onto an iron spar attached to the bow, and it took two hours to reach the side of the *Housatonic*, which was at anchor just outside Charleston Harbor. Small-arms fire from the *Housatonic* failed to stop the *Hunley*, which was just barely visible above the surface of the water. Once the torpedo (or mine) was rammed into the starboard side of the *Housatonic*, the submarine backed away. A lanyard was pulled that caused the torpedo to blow a hole in the side of the 207-ft-long *Housatonic*, and the Union blockade ship went down in five minutes with a loss of five lives. The *Housatonic* had enough time to release only two lifeboats into the water.

As the *Hunley* moved away, Dixon waved a blue magnesium light that was seen by Confederate soldiers at Battery Marshall—a signal that the *Hunley* had been successful in its mission and was ready to return to shore. However, Dixon and his crew disappeared without a trace, and it was assumed that the *Hunley* had sunk. Still, had the sailors become disoriented and headed farther out into the Atlantic? Had the Union gunboat that came in to rescue the survivors from the *Housatonic* bumped the submarine and caused it to go down? (The gunboat was arriving by the same route by which the *Hunley* was leaving, and there *is* a small amount of damage on the surface of the submarine today.) Had the sailors drowned, or had they been asphyxiated? And what were the identities of the sailors who undertook this dangerous mission?

Using his own money, Clive Cussler hired divers to search for the *Hunley*, and they towed a magnetometer behind a boat as they criss-crossed a grid, taking readings. The submarine was finally located in May 1995, after scores of other vessels had already been discovered. The water was just 27 ft deep, and the *Hunley* was buried under 3 ft of sand. Great quantities of sediment had to be suctioned away before the submarine could be exposed, and divers had to remove several more feet of sand to be able to get straps underneath the *Hunley* to lift it. A recovery team then used a crane barge to raise it to the surface on August 8, 2000. The director of the project was Robert Neyland, branch head of underwater archaeology for the Naval Historical Center, assisted by a large, specialized team of archaeologists, historians, conservators, and forensic scientists. Because the submarine was found outside the three-mile limit of the state of South Carolina but inside the 12-mile federal limit, the federal government (the U.S. Navy) now owns the craft. Thanks to negotiations by the late Senator Strom Thurmond, South Carolina has been granted the right to display the *Hunley* in perpetuity.

Upon recovery, the *Hunley* was taken to Clemson University's Warren Lasch Conservation Center on the old Charleston Navy Base, a former U.S. Navy warehouse, and here it is being conserved and displayed in a 90,000-gallon tank of fresh water maintained at 60 degrees Fahrenheit.

The *Hunley* currently leans at an angle of 45 degrees, the same angle at which it had come to rest on the harbor bottom. It will no doubt remain there in the conservation tank for years to come because its iron hull is still full of salts.

The actual opening and excavation of the interior of the *Hunley* began on January 21, 2001, and iron plates needed to be removed to get inside the hull. In the months that followed, the sediment was excavated with trowels, and the remains of the sailors were found, all of them still sitting at their original stations with no evidence that they had attempted to escape. It thus appears likely that they had been asphyxiated, rather than drowned, and recent studies of the submarine's pump system show that it had not been set to pump water out of the crew compartment, a further indication that the crew had not attempted to escape (Neely 2008–9: 7).

About 3,000 artifacts were found on board, and all artifacts are being conserved at the Warren Lasch Center. In the laboratory, plastic, water-filled tanks contain many pieces—such as the rudder—that are undergoing conservation. As tourists file by, and as Confederate reenactors proudly march about the facility, posing for tourist cameras, the project's conservators stabilize the remains in the laboratory. Headed by senior conservator Paul Mardikian and senior archaeologist Maria Jacobsen, the laboratory team has the necessary task of protecting the artifacts removed from inside this tightly sealed time capsule.

Certainly the most sensational of the artifacts taken from the submarine has been a $20 gold coin, dated 1860, that had been carried by Dixon himself. Given to him by his sweetheart, Queenie Bennett of Mobile, this good-luck piece had earlier saved Dixon's life at the Battle of Shiloh when a Union bullet bounced off the coin while it rested in a pocket of his trousers. That same dented coin was found in a pocket of one of the skeletons on board the *Hunley,* making Dixon the easiest of the sailors to be identified forensically. His remains were found in the forward section of the submarine, where he would have operated the rudder and the dive planes.

Other artifacts recovered have included buttons, eight tin canteens, pocket knives, watches, wallets, a beard comb, a thimble, a wooden smoking pipe that still had tobacco in it, an apothecary bottle, a sewing kit, a brass compass, garments from the crew members, and even the lantern that Dixon used to signal to compatriots on shore. Perhaps the most unexpected artifact found inside the *Hunley* was an identification tag ("dog tag") from a Union soldier, Ezra Chamberlin from Connecticut. After 136 years, it still hung around the neck of one of the skeletons, perhaps as a war souvenir.

The preservation on board the *Hunley* was so good that the bones of the sailors' feet were all still inside their boots. Intensive forensic studies were conducted on the sailors' bones, and brain tissue—much shrunken—was still intact inside the skulls. Genealogical research, coupled with forensics, ultimately permitted all eight crew members to be identified, and it was learned that George Dixon was accompanied by James Wicks, J. F. Carlsen, C. Lumpkin, Joseph Ridgaway, Frank Collins, Arnold Becker, and a man named "Miller." Facial reconstructions have been done for all eight, four of whom had actually been born in Europe. A morgue was maintained for the sailors in the Warren Lasch Conservation Center up until the end of the forensic work, and then all of the sailors' remains were reburied. On April 17, 2004, tens of thousands of tourists watched the final funeral procession for the crew of the *Hunley* as it made its way to Magnolia Cemetery in Charleston. More than 8,000 Civil War reenactors in blue and gray, as well as veiled widows in black, marched through downtown Charleston to honor the bravery of the Confederate dead.

While remembered for successfully sinking a Union ship, the *Hunley* stands out as a significant technological advance for its day (Smith 2000). Thanks to archaeology, it has been possible to determine that the submarine was very well built and possessed design elements that included a streamlined hull, an elliptical cross section, a clever ballast system, and dive planes that permitted the *Hunley* to move up and down in the water. The Civil War was, after all, a time of great technological innovation, and the *Hunley* was an exceptional vessel. The story of the *Hunley* is great and tragic at the same time, but as archaeology continues to unlock the secrets of the most successful submarine of the Civil War, eight Confederate sailors have returned to prominence, and the mystery of their demise has finally been solved.

7

Indian Wars in the American West

Expansion by white Americans into the western United States was often bloody as Native Americans were dispossessed from their traditional lands and increasingly confined to reservations. Treaties were frequently ignored as government officials, under pressure from business interests, sought to open larger areas to white settlement and facilitated the search for gold and other resources. Consequently there are hundreds of battle sites throughout the West and Southwest, the unfortunate result of the frequent conflicts among the U.S. Cavalry, Native Americans, and white settlers. None of these battles was more prominent than that at the Little Bighorn in Montana in 1876 (see "Case Study: The Battle of the Little Bighorn," page 82), but almost as famous was the Sand Creek Massacre in the Colorado Territory in 1864, at which time Colorado Volunteers slaughtered a great many Cheyenne and Arapaho.

The modern descendants of those who were victims of the Indian Wars have often requested that memorials be raised to honor those who fell, to remind modern visitors of broken promises and past injustices. Proof of site location is needed before the National Park Service can give "national historic site" recognition to any site, and it thus seems inevitable that archaeology will eventually be used to locate and memorialize most sites from the Indian Wars. However, given the sensitivity and recentness of these events, this research may sometimes prove to be painful for native descendants.

Research Projects

The U.S. government established numerous outposts from which to protect settlers and to ensure that native peoples would comply with government policies. In doing so, many frontier forts were established, and one of the first to be studied by archaeologists was Fort Bowie in southeastern Arizona, carefully stabilized and interpreted by the National Park Service. The original fort was established in 1862 and gradually expanded during the period of conflict with the Chiricahua Apaches (the 1860s through the 1880s). Fort Bowie was centrally involved in the conquest of the Apaches, and after the surrender of Geronimo in 1886, the fort gradually lost its utility and was totally abandoned by 1894.

It was after Fort Bowie was designated a national historic site (1964) that archaeology was conducted in a trash dump, leading to the recovery of some 17,000 artifacts from the late nineteenth century (Herskovitz 1978). The finds included some of the best available examples of military and civilian artifacts from any U.S. Army outpost, including such unexpected artifacts as perfume bottles, children's toys, fine ceramics, French plums, British ale, and Worcestershire sauce (Herskovitz 1978: 140).

In addition to its usefulness in reconstructing frontier forts, archaeology has been applied to several western battle sites of the nineteenth century, including the aforementioned Little Bighorn and Sand Creek, as well as the 1877 Battle of the Big Hole. Most of these sites are owned and protected by the National Park Service, so there has been a high level of federal involvement in presenting these battlefields to the public.

The exact location of the Sand Creek Massacre site has long since been forgotten, but history tells the story of how approximately 700–725 soldiers of the Colorado First and Third Volunteers under the command of Colonel John M. Chivington surprised a village of about 500 Cheyenne and Arapaho Indians, murdering at least 150 individuals as they were camped along Sand Creek in southeastern Colorado Territory. Over the course of November 29 and 30, 1864, soldiers killed Indians with howitzers and small-arms fire and then mutilated the bodies. After the army moved on, there was a public outcry and three federal investigations, and most Americans were shocked and sickened by what had occurred there.

In 1997 a metal-detector survey became the first archaeological effort to locate the massacre site, and then in 1998 Congress passed the Sand Creek Massacre National Historic Site Study Act. The National Park Service undertook a major research effort in 1998 and 1999 under the direction of Jerome Greene and Douglas Scott, and the Sand Creek Massacre Project successfully located the massacre site within the south bend of Sand Creek. Hundreds of artifacts were recovered that had been used by the Cheyenne and Arapaho, even as the team also found evidence for the soldiers who had killed them (Greene and Scott 2004; Scott 2003). Fresh historical research was conducted by Jerome Greene in diaries, firsthand accounts, and congressional reports, and this was followed by Douglas Scott's interviews with artifact collectors, by the examination of aerial photographs, and by Scott's analysis of artifact distribution patterns.

A key component of this research was that in 1999 the National Park Service carried out the extensive use of metal detectors to find the Indian village and to document the path of the attack:

> The research design specified that the inventory phase would em-
> ploy electronic metal detectors, visual survey methods, and piece-
> plot recording techniques as part of the standard archeological field-
> recording procedures. The purpose of these investigations was to
> locate and identify any archeological sites, features, or artifacts in
> the study area. The primary research goals were to determine if any
> physical evidence existed in the study boundary that could be as-
> sociated with the site of the Cheyenne and Arapaho village attacked
> by Chivington on November 29, 1864. (Greene and Scott 2004: 72)

With teams conducting metal-detector sweeps on the eastern edge of Sand Creek, they eventually discovered large quantities of ammunition, iron kettles, and tools from the 1860s. All finds were mapped in, and Greene and Scott ultimately verified that the site represented the 1864 camp of the Cheyenne peace chief, Black Kettle. The archaeology thus helped to bring about the establishment of the Sand Creek Massacre National Historic Site in 2000.

Douglas Scott also has been involved in locating and studying the 1877 Battle of the Big Hole, in which Nez Perce attempted to elude the Seventh U.S. Infantry while fleeing from Idaho to Canada. Several battle sites were created along the path of their flight, one of which was the Battle of the Big Hole site in southwestern Montana. Here the Seventh Infantry under Colonel John Gibbon attacked the Nez Perce camp, with both sides suffering numerous casualties before the remaining Nez Perce escaped to the east.

Modern research by Scott has successfully identified the soldiers' rifle pits, discovered many bullet concentrations, and even verified specific incidents from historical accounts of the battle: "The Nez Perce people accept the bullet clusters as definitive proof of their oral history, and archaeology has made this particular site even more important and sacred because it is proven at a level of reasonable scientific certainty" (Scott 2003: 59).

Examples of other western battle sites that have been intensively studied by archaeologists include remains from the Battle of Cieneguilla in 1854 and the Battle of Hembrillo in 1880. In both cases the U.S. Army fought against the Apache in what is now New Mexico. David Johnson, archaeologist with the USDA Forest Service, began in 2000 to study percussion caps, metal arrow points, and other artifacts at the Cieneguilla site to determine why mounted soldiers (dragoons) had suffered heavy casualties at the hands of the Apache. At the other battle site, Karl Laumbach studied clusters of cartridges at Hembrillo, beginning in 1989. Laumbach wanted to understand how the Ninth Cavalry had been able to defeat the Apache, even though the "Buffalo Soldiers" had been lured into a trap by Indians who held the high ground.

Once again, metal detectors were used to locate artifacts from these campaigns. This time 59 volunteers used metal detectors to cover 900 acres of battlefield. Hammer strike patterns on percussion caps were analyzed by Douglas Scott, helping him to identify the movement of individual weapons across the terrain. From a sample of 800 cartridges collected from Hembrillo, Scott was able to identify "145 different rifles or carbines and 39 different pistols. Because marks on the cartridges vary with the ejector mechanism of the weapon, he could even identify the make and model of the guns that fired them" (Laumbach 2001: 37).

Case Study: The Battle of the Little Bighorn

Arguably the most sensational and enduring story in the history of the American West is that of Lieutenant Colonel George Armstrong Custer and the Seventh U.S. Cavalry, fighting on the Little Bighorn River in the Montana Territory in the summer of 1876 (Fox 1988, 1991, 1993; Jordan 1986). The cavalry's defeat and deaths at the hands of Lakota (Western Sioux), Northern Cheyenne, and Arapaho warriors caused many generations of Americans to idolize the heroism of Custer and his men.

However, "Custer's Last Stand" was a romanticized version of a very ignominious defeat, and few stories of early America have required as much retelling as this one. In recent years "Custer's Last Stand" has evolved into the "Battle of the Little Bighorn," correctly reflecting the fact that there were two sides in this battle, and Northern Plains Indians were clearly the victors. Perceptions have obviously changed over time, and the 36-year-old Custer is now more likely to be remembered for his shortcomings, even as native peoples are remembered for their successful, if short lived, defense of their homeland.

In 1874 the Civil War was over, and white Americans were eager to continue their western movement, even though that meant Northern Plains Indians were increasingly pushed onto reservations, thus losing their traditional, nomadic way of life. In that year, the Seventh U.S. Cavalry and Custer—previously a major general and decorated hero in the Civil War—were assigned the task of keeping miners out of the Black Hills because of the discovery of gold on Indian land. However, keeping whites out had proven impossible. Conflict appeared inevitable once Sitting Bull and other war chiefs of the Lakota, Cheyenne, and Arapaho led their people off the Great Sioux Reservation, which had been assigned to them by the U.S. government. When ordered to return to the reservation before January 31, 1876, or face the U.S. Cavalry, Sitting Bull's people numbered between 5,000 and 7,000, of whom perhaps 1,500–2,000 were of warrior age.

The Seventh Cavalry was ordered to escort the Indians back onto their reservation. Once the cavalry had located the main Indian camp, Custer divided his command into three battalions, led by himself, Major Marcus A. Reno, and Captain Frederick W. Benteen. History documents that on June 25, 1876, Reno and a battalion of 120 men attacked Sitting Bull's huge summer camp, which ran for miles along the valley of the Little Bighorn River. A force of about 900 Lakota warriors rode out from the southern part of the village and outflanked Reno's command, but Reno survived after retreating and joining with Benteen's battalion.

Custer's own battalion turned north and traveled on to the vicinity of what is now known as Last Stand Hill. His soldiers picked the little hilltops and ridge lines as their defensive positions, but it was easy for Indians to approach them from all directions, through gullies and ravines, without being seen. This would have made it extremely difficult for Custer and his men to see the enemy's size or to follow their movements. It was there that the last 41 or so men out of five companies, totaling about 210 men, died with Custer in what was then considered to be the worst military loss since the Civil War. (About 268 died all together out of Custer's total command.) Crazy Horse was most likely the Indian leader who led the attack on Last Stand Hill, and the final battle probably lasted only one to two hours.

It has been estimated that 75–100 Indian warriors were also killed that day, an imprecise figure because the victors promptly removed their dead from the battlefield. We do not know where the Indian dead were subsequently buried, but the tribes broke camp after the battle and scattered as more U.S. Army columns approached. George Armstrong Custer died that day with several other members of his family: his brother Captain Thomas W. Custer, his brother Boston Custer, and a nephew, Autie Reed. At the request of his widow, Custer's body was later shipped east and then reburied at the U.S. Military Academy at West Point, where he had graduated last in the class of 1861.

The bodies of the soldiers and officers were initially buried where they had fallen, but in 1877 the remains of 11 officers and two civilians were shipped east, and in 1881 the enlisted men and scouts were dug up and reburied in a single mass grave on Last Stand Hill. Still later, in 1890, the U.S. Army placed headstone markers on the battlefield where each soldier had fallen, and even today about 40 white marble headstones on Last Stand Hill are a silent, moving tribute to the men of the Seventh Cavalry (figure 7.1). Most conspicuous is the single "black" stone in their midst, said to mark the spot where Custer's naked body was found after the battle (figure 7.2).

Because none of the soldiers with Custer had outlived this disaster, the only firsthand accounts of the battle on Last Stand Hill were those told from the Indian perspective, and some of these stories were collected many years later. It was generally believed that the soldiers had simply been outnumbered by a determined enemy that was much more familiar with the terrain.

The traditional accounts of the battle were told and retold, sometimes creating legends of heroism that were difficult to change. Custer's widow Elizabeth wrote the admiring book *Boots and Saddles* to honor and defend her slain husband (Custer 1885), and movies such as *They Died with Their Boots On* (1941), starring Errol Flynn as Custer, added to the already-enormous mythology surrounding the demise of the U.S. Seventh Cavalry.

Figure 7.1. Last Stand Hill at the Little Bighorn Battlefield. The white marble headstones mark the graves of soldiers and officers.

Figure 7.2. The headstones on Last Stand Hill. The black headstone in the middle marks the spot where George Armstrong Custer's body was found after the battle.

Tall prairie grass grew up over the site of the Little Bighorn Battlefield, renamed Little Bighorn Battlefield National Monument in 1991. This is located within what is today the Crow Indian Reservation in south-central Montana. No serious thought was given to the possibility of using archaeology to tell a more accurate story, and unfortunately, collectors over the years had removed huge numbers of artifacts from the battlefield. However, in the fall of 1983 a careless smoker dropped a cigarette, and the resultant prairie fire swept over 600 acres and instantly cleared the battle site of ground cover.

It was Richard Fox who suggested to the National Park Service that archaeology be conducted, and Douglas Scott, newly arrived at the Midwest Archeological Research Center in Lincoln, Nebraska, joined forces with Fox to carry out what became a highly original program of research. Together with experienced metal-detector operators, they formed a skirmish line and walked the field of battle, sweeping it with their metal detectors. Within the first hour, artifacts began to appear, and volunteers marked each find with a plastic flag. Trowels exposed the objects; every artifact was numbered, logged, and computerized; and detailed computer distribution maps were used to show how the battle had unfolded.

In the more than 20 years of research that followed, a host of armaments and bones (human and horse) were found upon the battlefield, including hundreds of bullets and cartridge casings, but only a very few metal arrowheads (Fox 1988; Scott and Fox 1987; Fox and Scott 1991; Scott et al. 1989). Over 5,000 artifacts were located in the vicinity of the battle, revealing that the Indians had used more than 47 different types of firearms and proving that this was principally a battle conducted with firearms (rather than more traditional Indian weapons).

Every time a spent cartridge was ejected and hit the ground, it left a distinctive strike pattern that is unique and that may be studied. Scott and Fox were able to follow some 350 weapons as they had been carried around the battlefield, in the process discovering huge numbers of cartridge cases at Indian sites. The Indians were well armed with repeating rifles, although they had some obsolete weapons too. The firing pin impression marks had made it possible to individualize a particular firearm. Other artifacts included buttons and clothing fasteners, but for Doug Scott, the most interesting find was a gold wedding band still encircling a human finger bone (Scott, personal communication, April 21, 2007). It is undeniable that "personal" artifacts such as this, the things that link us to the people of the past, always carry added meaning for researchers.

Recent archaeology at the Little Bighorn has changed long-held views about how the battle was fought. While we already knew from history that the Seventh Cavalry was equipped with .45-caliber Springfield single-shot carbines and Colt six-shot revolvers, we now know from forensic evidence that the Indians had over 200 repeating rifles, particularly Winchester and Henry rifles, that were superior to anything the soldiers carried. Not only did the Indians outnumber the U.S. Cavalry, but they were better armed and fought more effectively.

By connecting cartridges fired by the same gun, it is possible to trace troopers and warriors as they moved across the battlefield. Weapons fired by Indians were found to have been carried all over the battlefield, whereas troopers had moved very little. Clusters of cartridge cases suggest that troopers, rather than being spread out along skirmish lines as dictated by military manuals, were increasingly bunching together out of fear. On Last Stand Hill there was no valiant "last stand." Few soldiers' cartridge cases were found there, but there were *many* Indian bullets. The troopers were able to provide little resistance to overwhelming Indian firepower.

Today it is only a one- or two-minute walk from the National Park Service Visitors Center, with its exhibits and artifact collections, out to Last Stand Hill where the white marble markers and signboards help to tell the story. It is a hot and barren landscape, characterized by rolling prairie and scrub growth. While there are trees visible in the distance, there are none atop Last Stand Hill. Close to the Visitors Center is the National Cemetery where Major Reno lies, and just beyond Last Stand Hill is the new Indian Memorial, dedicated in 2003, which includes a sculpture of Spirit Warriors, those who were protecting the huge Indian camp when the Seventh Cavalry attacked.

The five-mile-long tour road that winds through Little Bighorn Battlefield National Monument runs past foxholes and rifle pits dug by soldiers with their spoons, cups, and knives because they did not have shovels with them. There are marble markers dedicated to "unknown" soldiers at many points along the tour road, illustrating the "running" nature of the battle, with soldiers dying in many places other than at Last Stand Hill. And there are signboards in the field describing the recent (post-1984) archaeology. This is a very rich, very archaeological landscape, and visitors cannot help but notice that the physical remains—and the story—go far beyond Last Stand Hill.

The demise of Custer and the Seventh Cavalry was shocking in 1876, with the defeat occurring soon after the opening of the nation's Centennial Exhibition, and it led to intense patriotic fervor and anti-Indian sentiment. Even today the Battle of the Little Bighorn continues to have an emotional impact upon audiences. And always there are questions: How did Custer actually die? Was Custer a brilliant commander or a reckless hothead who needlessly led his men to their deaths? Did Custer precipitate this disaster just for the sake of personal glory? Should Reno and Benteen have gone to Custer's aid, or was their wisest strategy to save their own battalions? Did Ulysses S. Grant, who hated Custer, and other senior officers deliberately send Custer to where they knew he would be killed? These and other questions that play up the "mystery" of the Little Bighorn have guaranteed a story that will forever be provocative. Indeed, the Little Bighorn has been termed the biggest historic attraction in the West, and now, thanks to archaeology, the events may be described with more accuracy than ever before.

8

Human Remains

Forensic archaeology, the excavation and plotting of human remains, works in concert with forensic anthropology, the analysis of human bones to determine age, sex, physical characteristics, stature, disease, pathologies, and cause of death. American battlefield sites frequently contain human remains—sometimes just a thin scatter of individual body parts that may resist all methods of detection—but frequently there are graves located nearby, often unmarked. Forts, on the other hand, more typically have associated cemeteries with marked graves, containing individuals who died from disease, noncombatant injuries, or battle-related trauma.

Marked graves have more legal protections, but no matter what the context, all human remains deserve respectful treatment and should be exhumed only when (1) there are pressing research questions, (2) there is the threat of destruction during construction or other earth-moving activities, (3) there is a risk of disturbance by treasure hunters, or (4) there is a legitimate "need to know" on the part of relatives or descendants. This last reason is especially important when dealing with human remains from recent military conflicts, cases where the recovery of remains is critical to bring closure to a grieving family. Respect for the dead and compassion for relatives of the deceased is clearly even more important than the desire by scholars to conduct new types of research.

Ongoing efforts to recover human remains from World War II sites and from Southeast Asia are well documented in the popular media, and we Americans are united in our desire to seek the return of all of our casualties from foreign wars. Crash sites from the Vietnam War period in Southeast Asia are recorded in the field just as rigorously as any other type of archaeological excavation.

Richard Gould in his recent book *Disaster Archaeology* (2007) has distinguished between "recovery" as it applies to (1) the physical recovery of human remains, and (2) the recovery that family and friends must go through after the loss of a loved one. The mass casualties that were the result of the attack upon the World Trade Center on September 11, 2001, reflected an entirely new type of war—the War on Terrorism—but mass casualties also result in commingled, mutilated human remains that are extremely difficult to identify and interpret. In cases such as this, the archaeological excavation of human remains, coupled with forensic analysis, has the potential to help families heal from the loss of their loved ones.

Forensic anthropology and archaeology have helped greatly in assigning an identity to forgotten soldiers and to the victims of war. Several recent studies have been especially effective in using soldiers' and officers' remains to better tell their stories, and examples are presented here from Snake Hill in Fort Erie, Ontario, the Little Bighorn in Montana, and Lake George in upstate New York. Also, it should be pointed out that not all combatants or victims of military campaigns are necessarily men. A woman who was one of the best-known victims of war is presented here (see "Case Study: The Murder and Scalping of Jane McCrea, the Heroine of Saratoga," page 99).

Research Projects

Snake Hill

One of the most exciting and informative exhumations of American soldiers' remains took place in Fort Erie, Ontario. Here in 1987 the bones of United States soldiers were discovered in a military graveyard dating to the War of 1812 (Pfeiffer and Williamson 1991). The soldiers had served as part of the garrison of Fort Erie after the American army captured it in the summer of 1814. The dead appear to have come from a field hospital, and they were but a small fraction of those who had died at Fort Erie. The international team of archaeologists and forensic scientists who worked on the bones discovered:

> Thirteen of the soldiers had broken bones that looked like projectile injuries. Seven had fractured thighs, two had fractured skulls, three had broken forearms (one had both broken), and there were broken ribs and shoulder bones as well. Altogether the physical anthropologists found fifty-three fractured bones among twenty-six complete

skeletons. The Snake Hill graveyard was a vivid testament to violent injury and death in wartime.

Most of the injuries appeared to come from shells, shrapnel, and cannonballs rather than small arms fire. . . . Between two and five hundred rounds of artillery fire rained down every twenty-four hours, killing or wounding about half a dozen men a day. . . . On one of the worst days, 27 August, there were more than twenty American casualties from the bombardment. (Litt, Williamson, and White-horne 1993: 108)

The Snake Hill cemetery at Fort Erie had more than its fair share of controversy because it was originally discovered at a building site where construction workers were backhoeing and dumping the bones. The rescue effort was further complicated by strong patriotic feelings on *both* sides of the border. Still, with good cooperation between the two nations, funding for the project was obtained, and museums, government agencies, the U.S. Army, and the Canadian army all participated in recovering and analyzing the bodies and the associated artifacts. Identifying the nationality of the soldiers was essential to their ultimate disposition, and there were plenty of buttons from American military uniforms in the graves. Virtually all of the 28 individuals in the graves were either definitely or probably American, and repatriation of military personnel killed and buried in foreign soil is an integral part of American military policy. Fortunately the project ended well when the 28 soldiers were returned to the United States for reburial in Bath National Cemetery at Bath, New York (reasonably close to the border and in an area from which many of the soldiers had originally been recruited).

The Little Bighorn

As presented in chapter 7, the Battle of the Little Bighorn site has provided extremely significant evidence for how that battle was fought on June 25, 1876, and that story is told at the National Park Service Visitors Center at the site. But the archaeology conducted between 1984 and 1989 also provided the impetus for examining the human remains that have been recovered from the battlefield. The bones of the men who rode and died with Custer have had a great deal to say about their ages, stature, health, and cause of death (Scott, Willey, and Connor 1998; Willey and Scott 1995).

Figure 8.1. Reconstructed faces of soldiers inside the National Park Service Visitors Center at the Little Bighorn Battlefield.

The forensic examination of the soldiers' bones has revealed blunt force trauma, sharp force trauma, cut marks, gunshot wounds, and evidence for multiple injuries to each body. History recorded that many of the soldiers' bodies had been badly mutilated, so much so that only 56 out of the 210 who died with Custer could be identified. Forensic anthropology has confirmed this; cut marks appear on many bones, and blunt force trauma shows faces were shattered from blows. In addition, sharp force trauma to the tops of skulls reveals scalping, and other cut marks demonstrate castration of the troopers by the Indians.

The troopers' average age, based on enlistment records, was 22, but their bones have revealed some of them to be as young as 16 or 17 years of age. Many of them were poor immigrants from western Europe, with an average height of 5 ft 7 in and an average weight of 150 lbs. Some of the troopers' faces have been reconstructed forensically (figure 8.1), and some have teeth that show black stains from extensive tobacco use. They had rheumatism and arthritis, and collapsed vertebrae suggest they must have had back problems from so much time spent in the saddle. On the whole, forensic anthropology reveals they may have been in rather poor condition when they arrived at the Little Bighorn.

Lake George, New York

The Village of Lake George, New York, had an extensive military occupation dating from about 1755 (the Battle of Lake George) and continuing intermittently until the American Revolution and beyond. No precise estimates exist for how many soldiers or civilians died during that period, but disease and injuries killed 500 or more members of the British garrison at Fort William Henry between 1755 and 1757, up to 200 or more were killed at the time of the so-called massacre in August 1757, and up to 1,000 or more died there in the mid-1770s, at which time Lake George was the center of the most extensive smallpox hospitals in the British colonies, with about 3,000 patients lying in hospitals in the village and on the heights at the south end of the lake (now the site of the Lake George Battlefield Park) (Starbuck 2002a). Out of perhaps 2,000 individuals who died in the community of Lake George during the mid- to late eighteenth century, few were buried with grave markers of any sort.

Throughout the nineteenth and twentieth centuries, it was a common occurrence for skeletons to be uncovered in the Village of Lake George, usually by chance. The only exception to this was the excavation of burials at Fort William Henry by Stanley Gifford in the mid-1950s, at which time he deliberately sought and then exposed 10 skeletons at one corner of the fort's military cemetery as well as scattered skeletal remains throughout the charred ruins of the fort (figure 8.2) (Starbuck 1993, 2002; Steegmann and Haseley 1988). These were reanalyzed in 1993 (figure 8.3), and another eight grave shafts were exposed in 1995 by Brenda Baker and Maria Liston. At that time, three more skeletons were fully excavated by anthropologists (Liston and Baker 1995; Baker and Rieth 2000).

The undisturbed cemetery at Fort William Henry is extremely rich in information about some of the injuries and diseases that affected soldiers at the time of the French and Indian War, and human remains in the cemetery are revealing about the overall state of their health. Especially noticeable within the assemblage of skeletons are herniated disks from soldiers who carried loads that were much too heavy, but the bones also reveal evidence for wear and tear on their joints, and for arthritis, infections, and abscessed teeth (Starbuck 2002: 63). Muscles in the back had torn away from the bones, and ribs had become fused to the vertebrae.

To this may be added evidence for several types of trauma, including decapitations, cut marks in the chest and stomach areas, gashes suggesting

Figure 8.2. Stanley Gifford exposing soldiers' skeletons in 1957 inside the so-called crypt at Fort William Henry. This had been a casemate or cellar room, and five victims of the massacre had been placed here but only four skulls. (Courtesy of the Fort William Henry Museum.)

genital mutilation, and indications that a number of men had been shot with musket balls, especially in the knee (Liston and Baker 1995). Some showed evidence for diseases such as tuberculosis, although some diseases—such as smallpox—acted so quickly that no traces were left on the bones. Also, fly pupae were found within the cloth of some of the burials, "indicating that these bodies were left unburied for at least several days" (Baker and Rieth 2000: 57). Life at this frontier outpost was harsh, if the bones are to be believed.

Skeletons have been found in other locations within the Village of Lake George, including some in the Mohican Street area where, in the late nineteenth century, Dr. James Cromell "while digging cellars for his house (1860) and vault for ice-house (1867) exhumed thirteen skulls" (Bellico 1995: 289). Often the remains of soldiers are discovered purely by chance. An example of this occurred on May 16, 2001, when a human skull was unearthed in a backhoe trench on Mohican Street during routine maintenance conducted on a gas main by the Niagara Mohawk Power Corporation. The backhoe had detached the skull, mandibles, and the first three

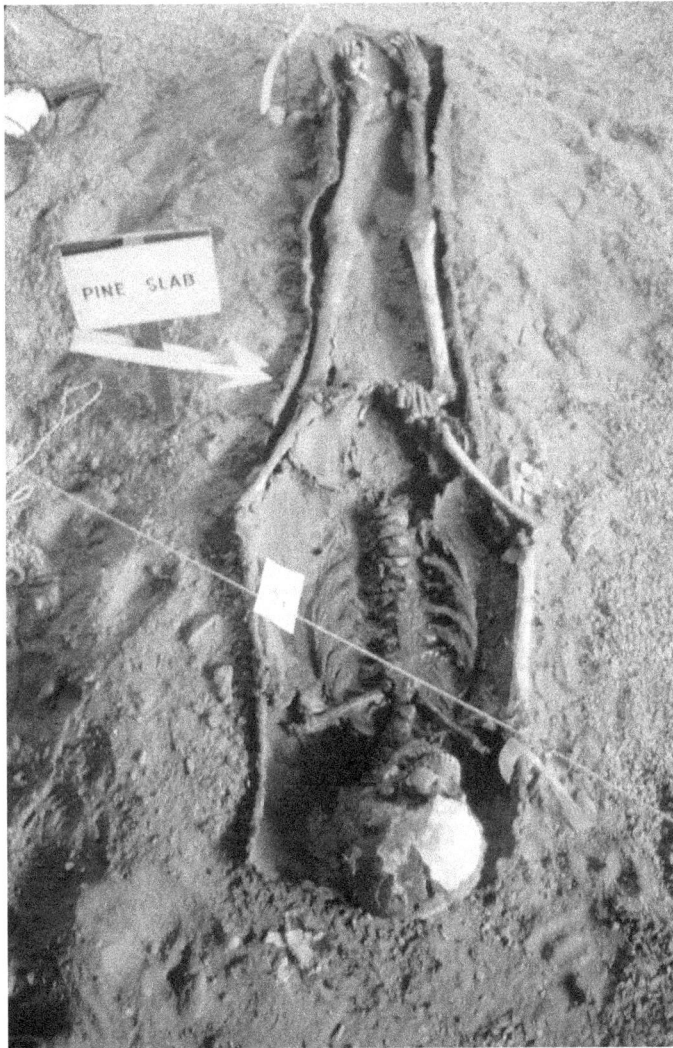

Figure 8.3. One of the soldiers' skeletons exposed in the military cemetery at Fort William Henry, discovered on top of a slab of pine bark (which had originally been used to carry the individual to the cemetery).

Figure 8.4. A soldier's skeleton discovered inside a modern utility trench on Mohican Street in Lake George, New York.

cervical vertebrae from the skeleton, but the remainder of the skeleton was articulated and revealed that the individual had been buried on his back with his arms straight out at his sides (i.e., an extended burial). Work was halted immediately, the Warren County Sheriff's Department was contacted, and in turn a sheriff's deputy called me and asked if I would expose and document the skeleton.

With a few hundred onlookers, and assisted by Warren County Coroner Paul Bachman, I spent the day scraping the north wall of the backhoe trench (which was closest to the skull) with a trowel, looking for evidence of a burial shaft or a coffin. Finding none, I expanded the excavation throughout the course of the afternoon until it could be determined that all bones had been found (figure 8.4). In doing so, I exposed the upper torso of a young Caucasian male who presented evidence of cuts and blows to the skull. Based on his teeth and cranial sutures, he was probably no more than about 20 years of age at time of death, and the length of his left femur (about 49 cm long) suggested that his maximum stature was about 70 in (5 ft 10 in).

In examining the surviving upper torso and cranium of the skeleton, it is possible to make several likely interpretations. First, given its location near Fort William Henry, this was probably a young, eighteenth-century soldier. In the absence of associated artifacts, it is impossible to state whether he lived and died during the French and Indian War or the Revolutionary War (or during the period between the wars). It is also impossible to say whether he was British or French. He was fairly tall and robust, probably reasonably healthy (given the condition of his teeth, which was quite good for that time period), and he appears to have been buried with little or no clothing and without benefit of a coffin. This was not surprising because a great many soldiers of the French and Indian War were buried in nothing more than a sheet, and uniforms were then reused by others.

Once completely exposed, I drew the skeleton and photographed it in situ. We then slid a sheet of plywood underneath what remained of the skeleton, and it was removed to the coroner's office. The bones were subsequently turned over to a local funeral home for reburial in a small casket. The reburial took place on the grounds at Fort William Henry, next to the cemetery that had been excavated by Stanley Gifford in the 1950s. Both a priest and a minister presided over the burial service.

It was not until after the partial skeleton had been turned over to the funeral home and the loose dirt cleaned off that it was noticed the individual had most likely been scalped. The skull had two prominent, deep cut marks along the hair line on the frontal bone, and there were two long, deep cuts running down the front and the rear of the left parietal bone, suggesting that the person had received severe knife or sword cuts to the left side of the head. Finally, there were two deep depressions (blunt trauma), also on the left parietal bone, indicating that he had taken some very heavy blows to the side of the head. It is impossible to say which of these marks reflects the fatal blow or cut that killed him.

In the past in Lake George, when skeletons like this were encountered, they no doubt were often discarded or ignored by workmen or developers who did not want their projects slowed or stopped. It was fortunate that in this case the work crew did stop and notified authorities, leading to a respectful reinterment several days later as a large Memorial Day crowd observed the proceedings.

What Not to Do

On June 5, 2006, the Associated Press announced "Skeletons found at Army Ranger Site": "A husband and wife team of amateur archaeologists have unearthed human skeletons, believed to be about 250 years old, at a burial site here on the Hudson River island that's considered the birthplace of today's U.S. Army Rangers" (Carola 2006).

Today most Americans have a very strong sense that it is inappropriate for the public, or even well-trained professionals, to dig up the dead solely for reasons of curiosity. But this recent press release, carried in newspapers across the United States, presented news that was almost a throwback to the days when collectors were able to rob graves without serious consequences. True, artifact collecting continues unabated, but the destruction of graves has been greatly reduced as the general public, and state legislators, have decided that the looting of graves should not take place in any civilized society. Yet here, in Fort Edward, New York, a pair of looters had been quietly unearthing the graves of soldiers or rangers from the French and Indian War and keeping the story quiet until they were ready to call the Associated Press to get maximum "credit" for their discovery.

As more details came out, the story grew much worse. The diggers, who definitely were *not* archaeologists, had made their initial discovery many months before after using power equipment to remove several feet of overburden. They had even notified local village police of what they were doing in the fall of 2005, but only after they had concluded weeks of digging. After being told not to do anything further without contacting the police again, and not to proceed without professionals doing the work, they boldly resumed digging in the spring of 2006. They continued to keep the discoveries quiet until they were ready to "go public." By the time they called the Associated Press, they had discovered and desecrated a total of eight skeletons, together with buttons and the stains from many other graves, estimated to be as many as two hundred. Curiously enough, the looters were even naming the skeletons (e.g., "Caleb" and "Sammy") as they tried to imitate what they had seen professional archaeologists do.

When the police and the county district attorney told them to stop, they initially refused, arguing that it was private property and they had been given permission to dig by the property owner. What this unfortunately highlights is that the cemetery laws in most states protect those within marked cemeteries, as well as the graves of those identified as Native Americans, but the unmarked graves of Caucasians or African Americans do not always share the same protections. This is especially true in the cases of those from America's early wars, who often died in large numbers far from home, sometimes causing them to be buried in unmarked mass graves or in rows of individual graves.

I was first informed of the Fort Edward situation on my cell phone as I was walking across the Mississippian site of Cahokia in Illinois. What followed were several days of phone calls, police visits to the perpetrators, and growing frustration by the district attorney as we all realized how weak New York state law can be in protecting unmarked graves. The district attorney finally made phone calls to see whether the New York State Museum would consider sending in a team to clean up the mess and record the remains. That was ultimately what happened, in mid-July, and in the end no one was fined or thrown in jail.

The site was covered over, but the treasure hunters had had their names and pictures splashed across the newspapers and evening television news programs for days, which was exactly what they wanted. Because the property owner had allowed the inappropriate digging, there was nothing that the professional community could do. Clearly none of this should have happened, but it does point out the need to have tougher burial laws, especially in cases where soldiers' graves are at risk. We can only hope that the remains of our nation's soldiers are never again unearthed for such attention-getting purposes.

Case Study: The Murder and Scalping of Jane McCrea, the Heroine of Saratoga

Most accounts of forts and battlefields have very little to say about the women who lived on the frontier, and that is especially true for the military conflicts of the seventeenth and eighteenth centuries (Starbuck 1994). However, one story stands out, and that is the infamous murder and scalping of Miss Jane McCrea, a young woman of Scottish descent who was betrothed to a Tory officer traveling with General John Burgoyne's army in the summer of 1777. Jane McCrea had been born in Bedminster, New Jersey, the daughter of a Presbyterian minister, and she later relocated to the town of Fort Edward, New York, where her family was divided in its loyalties: Some favored the British Crown, and others clearly preferred independence from their mother country. Jane's own loyalties are unknown, although her betrothal to a Loyalist, David Jones, would suggest that she may have been friendly to the Crown.

By July 1777, a 23- or 24-year-old Jane McCrea had come to reside in the home of Sarah McNeil in Fort Edward, and they both were awaiting the arrival of Jones and the British army. The rest of the community had already fled south toward Albany, fearing the Indians that accompanied Burgoyne's army. Farmsteads had been attacked, settlers killed and scalped, and Burgoyne was already being criticized for using "terror tactics" to enforce loyalty to the Crown. Some accounts suggest that Jane was even wearing her wedding dress in anticipation of marriage that day to her fiancé.

Events took an ominous turn when Burgoyne sent out a party of Indians to escort the two women back to his camp, and the scouting party literally dragged both women by their hair from the cellar of Sarah McNeil's house. Jane was mounted on a horse, while Sarah walked, and a short distance later Jane was killed and scalped. When the long, beautiful hair arrived in the British camp—the Indians expected a bounty for the scalp—it was immediately recognized by David Jones, and Jane's body was recovered and buried.

Accounts differed at the time as to the cause of Jane's death, with the Indians claiming that a musket ball fired by colonial forces had actually killed her, while the British and Americans believed that two parties of Indians had clashed over Jane because each wanted the reward for escorting her back to camp. Sarah McNeil survived the raid and subsequently lived another 22 years, passing away in 1799 of natural causes at the age of 77, one of the wealthiest women in the region.

The death of Jane McCrea and the disposition of her remains might have been just one more tragic event on the American frontier, except that the story of her death was successfully trumpeted by colonial leaders who used her death as a recruitment device to increase opposition to the British Crown. Over the next few months, many thousands of Americans enlisted to fight against the British at the Battle of Saratoga. Jane became a highly visible symbol of colonial resistance and thus posthumously earned the nickname of the "Heroine of Saratoga." Given the conflicting accounts of her death, the lack of solid evidence for her appearance, and the notoriety of her hair as the most famous scalp of the eighteenth century, Jane's body and her grave continued to be a source of curiosity in the centuries that followed.

Hoping to remove some of the mystery, I contacted her oldest living relative in May 2002 and requested family permission to open her grave. (Her current grave is actually her third grave site in Fort Edward.) Modern forensic techniques appeared to have the potential to reveal more about her cause of death and her appearance, but historical sources suggested that much of her skeleton may have been removed in 1852 by souvenir hunters.

I assembled a team of forensic scientists and archaeologists, and my attorney submitted a petition to the Supreme Court of Washington County, New York. Forensic investigations invariably require specialists from several fields, including anthropologists, archaeologists, genealogists, historians, radiologists, and law enforcement personnel. We were subsequently issued a court order allowing us to enter the grave, and on April 9, 2003, about two dozen scholars and police gathered with me at the graveside at 6:00 a.m.

Our first step was to erect a tent around the exhumation site to ensure privacy for any human remains that might be found—this was required by our court order—and we proceeded to remove the limestone monument from atop the grave. The excavation continued until we found the dark stain of the grave shaft (figure 8.5), and by the end of the day we had found what we were looking for and more (Starbuck 2004, 2006). There actually were two skeletons in the grave, Jane McCrea as well as the more robust skeleton of a very elderly woman. Both sets of bones, but only one skull (that of the older woman), had been packed into a box that measured no more than 20 × 24 in × 9 in deep. Since these were secondary burials, not placed in the grave until after the flesh was gone, the "bone box" had been no larger than necessary.

Because it was one of the primary catalysts leading up to the Battle of Saratoga, the death of Jane McCrea contributed to the first great American victory of the Revolutionary War. Fortunately, the U.S. Department of Defense agreed at the inception of this project to prepare mitochondrial DNA (mtDNA) profiles for the bones of both women. Dr. Anthony Falsetti, head of the C. A. Pound Laboratory at the University of Florida at Gainesville, oversaw the forensic anthropology conducted on the bones; and Dr. Lowell Levine, an odontologist who is codirector of the New York State Police Forensic Investigation Center, was present to analyze any teeth that might be found in the grave. While Jane McCrea had never married and left no direct descendants that could supply us with a comparative mtDNA sample, her elderly companion, Sarah McNeil, had been married twice and did have children.

Genealogical research revealed a seventh-generation maternal descendant for Sarah, and acting on a hunch, we collected a modern mtDNA sample from that descendant. The Department of Defense compared it to

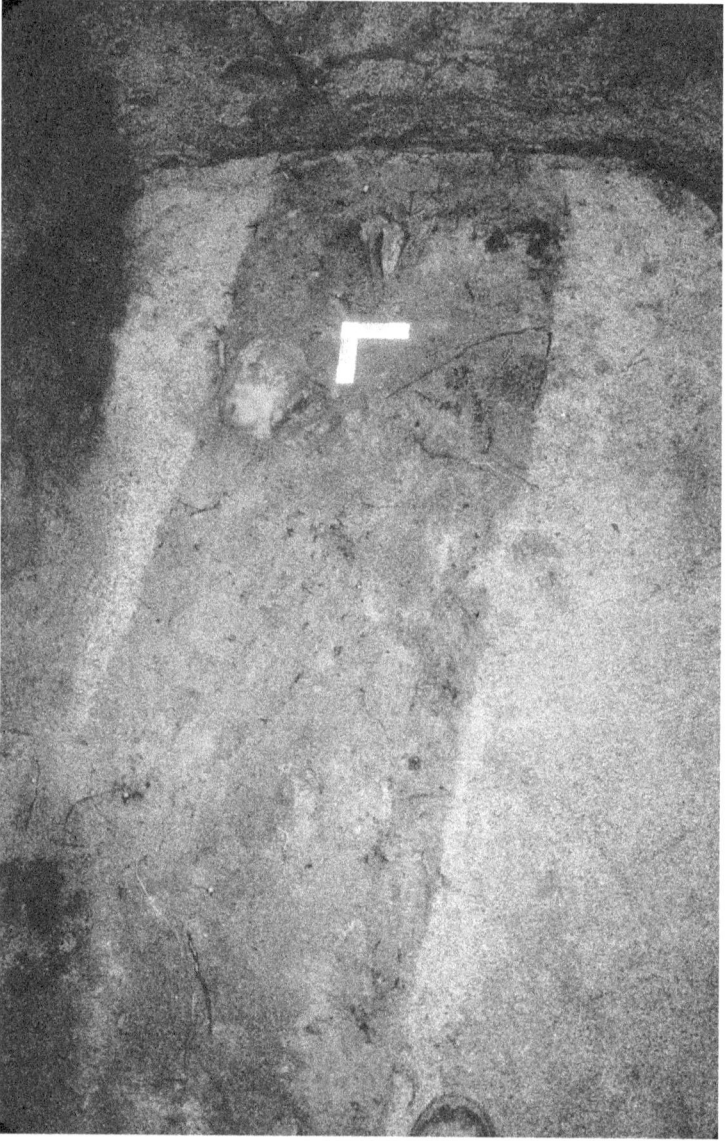

Figure 8.5. This dark stain in Union Cemetery marks the outline of the grave containing the remains of Jane McCrea and Sarah McNeil. The skull of Sarah McNeil is visible just to the left of the scale.

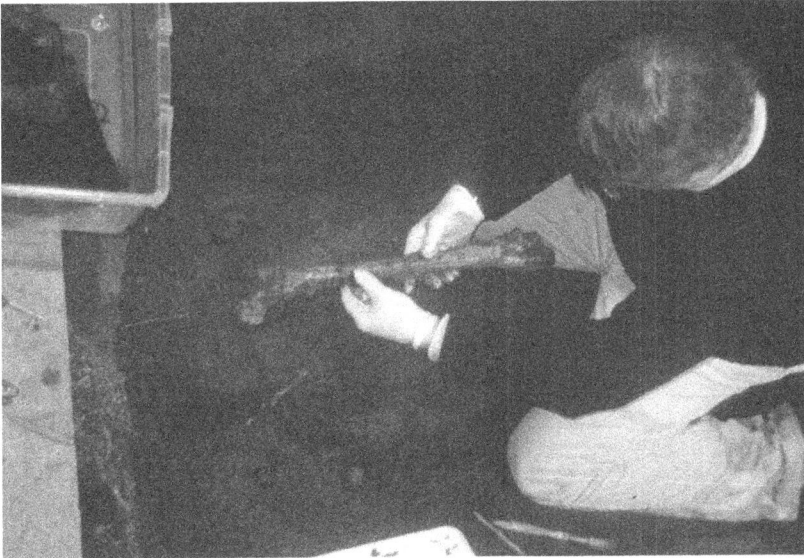

Figure 8.6. David Starbuck is working inside the grave shaft in Union Cemetery and is holding one of the femurs of Jane McCrea. The latex gloves were worn to prevent contamination of the mtDNA sample.

the ancient mtDNA profile prepared for the bones of the elderly woman, and the profiles matched. The modern mtDNA and the ancient mtDNA revealed that Sarah's and Jane's bones had been combined in death, and both had been moved to their current cemetery location in 1852. Some years later, a local newspaper, the *Ray*, reported on March 14 and March 20, 1887, that the box containing Jane McCrea's bones had been "broken open and nearly all the bones stolen" and her bones were "scattered over the country." Some of her bones may well have been taken, but now, thanks to archaeology, it has been demonstrated that the bones of Sarah McNeil were added to the coffin.

Two sets of relatives now had an interest in the remains, and it was necessary to petition for another court order and go back into the grave in 2005 to do a thorough separation of the two skeletons. Each woman could now be given her own coffin and her own grave. According to Dr. Falsetti's measurements, Jane had been petit, no more than 5 ft 0 in to 5 ft 4 in, while Sarah was a very robust 5 ft 6 in to 5 ft 10 in. Given their differences in age and stature, the separation of their two skeletons was quite straightforward. The more porous, spongy (cancellous) bones of Jane's skeleton had disintegrated, but her long bones and most of her pelvis, clavicles, and scapulae had survived (figure 8.6). Sarah's skeleton was somewhat less complete—one leg was missing as well as the cancellous bones—and all teeth were missing from her jaws. The immediate impression she conveyed was of a very elderly individual. Unfortunately, with Jane's skull missing, it is impossible to state what her features looked like, or what her cause of death may have been. Sarah's face, on the other hand, was recreated by Herbert Buckley, a leading facial reconstruction expert who works for the New York State Police Forensic Investigation Center, and we were able to show Sarah's "face" to some of her descendants before both women were reburied on April 16, 2005.

Our work was not without controversy. A host of letters to the editor appeared in local newspapers, decrying our efforts to disturb a local icon, and the village's mayor announced that Fort Edward would "lose its history" if we were allowed to proceed. In some quarters there was terror that we would find Jane McCrea was *not* in the grave and all the myths spawned over 226 years would have to be changed.

Hundreds of signatures in opposition to our exhumation were collected on a petition that was submitted to the court, political cartoons were published, and protestors invaded the cemetery on the day of the first exhumation. Fortunately, all of their efforts failed. After all, we were determined to proceed, to replace folklore with modern science. But more to the point, our research was supported by Jane McCrea's relatives, and that was the most important factor in the court of law. Our study would have ended immediately had not her relatives been in support of this research.

In a great many cases, forensic analysis has played an enormous role in "bringing back" the victims of warfare in earlier centuries, but this was a case where early American women—those who have most often been neglected by traditional history—had important stories to tell. The skeletal remains of Jane and Sarah have helped give them back a part of their identity, and archaeology has now added yet another chapter to the Battle of Saratoga, that of two women who were victimized during the events that led up to the battle.

Final Thoughts

These are just a sampling of the forensics cases in which modern analytical techniques have been employed to recover and interpret the remains of soldiers from America's early wars. This type of work invariably excites the public and draws media attention, but clearly in most instances human remains should be left undisturbed unless threatened with road construction, urban renewal, or other earth-moving activities that might dislodge bones from their intended resting place. Still, a family's need to know and the opportunity to ask meaningful questions has often sparked innovative research, and clearly forensics work by well-trained professionals has the potential to add to our knowledge of those who served in the military.

9

Reflections on the Past and the Future

America's forts and battlefields are able to provide a deeply satisfying experience to modern visitors, and there is nothing that quite matches the excitement that comes from peering over the walls of a fort, entering a subterranean prison that once held military captives, viewing reenactors in an encampment (figure 9.1), or walking the lines of a battlefield and trying to imagine the strategies employed as troops lined up to face each other and the enemy's cannons. Nearly every state has excellent military sites that may be visited. Some of these are included within our National Park System, others are owned and managed by state or local agencies, and some are privately owned.

It would be unfair to identify any of these as the "best" sites to visit because what inspires each of us is a very personal matter, determined in large measure by (1) whether we had ancestors who served at that fort or battlefield, (2) the fort or battlefield's siting (a fort overlooking a lake or the ocean is very grand indeed), (3) the knowledge we carry with us to the site (some background research guarantees a much better visitor experience), and (4) the integrity of what has survived. A visit to an early fort is much more impressive when we know that *everything* we are looking at is original, albeit with some minor concessions to stabilization and interpretation.

It thus is important to know when the public presentation at a given site has a solid basis in archaeological excavation or survey work. The accuracy of a reconstruction, signage, and dioramas in a visitors' center are all critical to the impressions we carry away with us, and it is comforting when we know that archaeology has been used effectively as a prelude to reconstruction.

The "must see" sites surely include the Spanish forts at St. Augustine in Florida, James Fort in Virginia, Fort Michilimackinac in Michigan, Fort

Figure 9.1. French and Indian War reenactors camped in 2007 at the southern end of Lake George, New York. This event was held to commemorate the 250th anniversary of the massacre at Fort William Henry.

Ticonderoga in New York, the Gettysburg Battlefield and Valley Forge in Pennsylvania, and the Little Bighorn Battlefield in Montana. However, many hundreds of other military sites are also available for public viewing, and all have the potential to tell meaningful stories to visitors.

Regrettably, a great many of the national parks that contain military sites—and have made extensive use of archaeology—do not even mention archaeology in their exhibits. On the other hand, there are many state parks throughout the United States that *do* feature archaeology prominently throughout their interpretive programs. Perhaps this, too, should be a factor in determining which sites are worth visiting.

Looking back over many years of research, it was between the 1930s and the 1960s that the most intensive military site excavations were conducted, usually as a prelude to reconstruction. Today a heightened sensitivity to the needs of historic preservation has greatly reduced the scale of most projects. After all, forts are not a renewable resource, and too many of America's military sites have already been overdug. However, there are still dozens of research-oriented excavations every summer, most often seeking details about the daily lives of ordinary soldiers, and virtually all state- and federally owned forts and battlefields require archaeological testing whenever there are below-ground disturbances.

So it is that military sites archaeology continues to be one of the most exciting subfields of historical archaeology, a field that generates enormous popular interest among the general public, especially the many thousands of visitors every summer to America's forts and battlefields. *The Archaeology of Forts and Battlefields* is a topic that will forever be fresh and relevant as we marvel at the hardships faced by early armies, wonder at the "what ifs" of every military campaign, and reanalyze the strategies and tactics of every battle, siege, and maneuver. What were the strategies that determined a battle would occur in a particular place? How did the military decide where to build each fort or entrenchment? These questions and others cannot always be answered, but thanks to the techniques of modern archaeology, we are able to tell the stories and appreciate the life experiences of thousands of soldiers and officers who, much like soldiers today, were thrown into unfamiliar settings and adapted as best they could in order to survive.

Warfare has always been a huge part of the American experience, and that continues to be the case today as we fight foreign wars and debate the moral consequences at home. Some of us dreamed about being soldiers when we were children—I certainly did—while others have actually served in combat and still other Americans passionately re-create the lives of early soldiers by portraying them at reenactments. I believe that something we all share is a desire to draw close to the places where past wars were fought and where early fortifications were erected. It is distinctively American to want to identify with those who served in America's early wars, and I believe that it is at least partially through national pride that we archaeologists want to discover the foundation stones and stains from past wars, to recover and analyze the artifacts that soldiers once held and later lost, and to tell their stories as accurately as we possibly can.

Every nation has archaeological sites that bring equal measures of excitement and learning, but for Americans, our nation was born and tempered in conflict among peoples of many different cultures. Our forts and battlefields are a potent visual reminder of what our ancestors went through to create the unified nation we are today. All of these military sites are capable of adding to our knowledge, and today's archaeologists are using innovative analytical techniques to help America's forts and battlefields come alive for modern audiences.

Bibliography

Adams, Diane L. 1989. *Lead Seals from Fort Michilimackinac, 1715–1781*. Archaeological Completion Report Series No. 14. Mackinac State Historic Parks, Mackinac Island, MI.

Anburey, Thomas. 1969 [1789]. *Travels Through the Interior Parts of America*. London: William Lane. New York: New York Times & Arno Press.

Anderson, Fred. 2000. *Crucible of War*. New York: Vintage Books.

———. 2005. *The War that Made America*. New York: Viking.

Arana, Luis Rafael, and Albert Manucy. 2005. *The History of Castillo de San Marcos*. St. Augustine, FL: Historic Print & Map.

Archaeology Magazine. The Archaeology of War. 2005. Long Island City, NY: Hatherleigh Press.

Arkush, Elizabeth N., and Mark W. Allen, eds. 2006. *The Archaeology of Warfare: Prehistories of Raiding and Conquest*. Gainesville: University Press of Florida.

Babits, Lawrence E. 1988. "Military Records and Historical Archaeology." In *Documentary Archaeology in the New World*, ed. Mary C. Beaudry, pp. 119–125. New York: Cambridge University Press.

———. 1995. "Bullets from the Maple Leaf." *Military Collector and Historian* 47(3):119–126.

———. 2010. "Documents and Digging to Reconstruction: 1756 Fort Dobbs, NC." Paper presented to the 43rd Annual Conference on Historical and Underwater Archaeology, Jacksonville, FL.

Baker, Brenda J., and Christina B. Rieth. 2000. "Beyond the Massacre: Historic and Prehistoric Activity at Fort William Henry." *Northeast Anthropology* 60:45–61.

Baldwin, Colonel Jeduthan. 1906. *The Revolutionary Journal of Col. Jeduthan Baldwin 1775–1778*. Bangor, ME: Printed for the De Burians.

Beaudet, Pierre, and Celine Cloutier. 1989. *Archaeology at Fort Chambly*. Parks Canada Studies in Archaeology, Architecture and History. Ottawa: National Historic Parks and Sites Branch, Parks Canada. Translated from original French text.

Bellico, Russell P. 1995. *Chronicles of Lake George: Journeys in War and Peace*. Fleischmanns, NY: Purple Mountain Press.

Bevan, Bruce, David G. Orr, and Brooke S. Blades. 1984. "The Discovery of the Taylor House at the Petersburg National Battlefield." *Historical Archaeology* 18(2):64–74.

Bingeman, John M., and Arthur T. Mack. 1997. "The Dating of Military Buttons: Second Interim Report Based on Artefacts Recovered from the 18th Century Wreck *Invincible*, Between 1979 and 1990." *International Journal of Nautical Archaeology* 26(1):39–50.

Bradley, Robert L. 1981. *The Forts of Maine, 1607–1945: An Archaeological and Historical Survey*. Augusta: Maine Historic Preservation Commission.

Bradley, Robert L., and Helen B. Camp. 1994. *The Forts of Pemaquid, Maine: An Archaeological and Historical Study*. Occasional Publications in Maine Archaeology 10. Augusta: Maine Historic Preservation Commission.

Brain, Jeffrey P. 1995. *Fort St. George: Archaeological Investigation of the 1607–1608 Popham Colony on the Kennebec River in Maine*. Salem, MA: Peabody Essex Museum.

———. 1997. *Fort St. George II: Continuing Investigation of the 1607–1608 Popham Colony on the Kennebec River in Maine*. Salem, MA: Peabody Essex Museum.

———. 1998. *Fort St. George III: 1998 Excavations at the Site of the 1607–1608 Popham Colony on the Kennebec River in Maine*. Salem, MA: Peabody Essex Museum.

———. 1999. *Fort St. George IV: 1999 Excavations at the Site of the 1607–1608 Popham Colony on the Kennebec River in Maine*. Salem, MA: Peabody Essex Museum.

———. 2000. *Fort St. George V: 2000 Excavations at the Site of the 1607–1608 Popham Colony on the Kennebec River in Maine*. Salem, MA: Peabody Essex Museum.

———. 2001. *Fort St. George VI: 2001 Excavations at the Site of the 1607–1608 Popham Colony on the Kennebec River in Maine*. Salem, MA: Peabody Essex Museum.

———. 2007. *Fort St. George: Archaeological Investigation of the 1607–1608 Popham Colony on the Kennebec River in Maine*. Occasional Publications in Maine Archaeology No. 12. Augusta: Maine State Museum, Maine Historic Preservation Commission, and Maine Archaeological Society.

Brose, David. 1966. "Excavations in Fort Mackinac, 1965." *Michigan Archaeologist* 12(2):88–101.

Brown, Margaret Kimball. 1971. "Glass from Fort Michilimackinac: A Classification System for Eighteenth Century Glass." *Michigan Archaeologist* 17(3–4):97–215.

Calver, William Louis, and Reginald Pelham Bolton. 1950. *History Written with Pick and Shovel*. New York: New-York Historical Society.

Campbell, Lt. Col. J. Duncan. 1958. "Investigations at the French Village 1957." *Bulletin of the Fort Ticonderoga Museum* 10(2):143–155.

———. 1965. "Military Buttons: Long-lost Heralds of Fort Mackinac's Past." *Mackinac History* 1: 7. Mackinac Island State Park Commission, Mackinac Island, MI.

———. 1967. "Military Sites." *Historical Archaeology* 1:38–40.

Carola, Chris. 2006. "Skeletons Found at Army Ranger site." Press release from the Associated Press, Albany, NY, June 5.

Catton, Bruce. 1965. *A Stillness at Appomattox*. New York: Pocket Books.

Chaney, Edward, and Kathleen A. Deagan. 1989. "St. Augustine and the La Florida Colony . . ." In *First Encounters*, ed. Jerald T. Milanich and Susan Milbrath, pp. 166–182. Gainesville: University Press of Florida.

Coe, Michael D. 2006. *The Line of Forts: Historical Archaeology on the Colonial Frontier of Massachusetts*. Hanover: University Press of New England.

Cohn, Michael. 1983. "Evidence of Children at Revolutionary War Sites." *Northeast Historical Archaeology* 12:40–42.

Cooper, James Fenimore. 1980 [1826]. *The Last of the Mohicans*. New York: Penguin Books.

Cotter, John L. 1958. *Archeological Excavations at Jamestown Colonial National Historical Park and Jamestown National Historic Site Virginia*. Archeological Research Series 4. National Park Service, Washington, DC.

Cranmer, Leon. 1993. "Fort Halifax Archaeological Excavations 1991." *Maine Archaeological Society Bulletin* 33(2):23–31.

Cranmer, Leon, and Anne Hilton. 1987. "'It Stood Its Ground Until . . . ': The Archaeological Excavations at Fort Halifax." *Kennebec Proprietor* 4(4):21–24.

Cruson, Daniel. 2001. "The Archaeology of an Enlisted Man's Hut at Putnam Memorial State Park." *Bulletin of the Archaeological Society of Connecticut* 63:41–58.

Cruson, Daniel, and Kathleen von Jena. 2002. "The Different Lives of Officers and Enlisted Men at the Redding Winter Encampment of 1778–1779." *Bulletin of the Archaeological Society of Connecticut* 64:55–68.

Custer, Elizabeth Bacon. 1885. *Boots and Saddles, or Life in Dakota with General Custer*. New York: Harper & Brothers.

Deagan, Kathleen, and Darcie MacMahon. 1995. *Fort Mose: Colonial America's Black Fortress of Freedom*. Gainesville: University Press of Florida/Florida Museum of Natural History.

Deetz, James. 1977. *In Small Things Forgotten: An Archaeology of Early American Life*. Garden City, NY: Anchor Press/Doubleday. Rev. ed., 1996.

Desany, Jessica R. 2008. "The Enshrining of Fort Ste. Anne." *SAA Archaeological Record* 8(1):29–32.

Evans, Lynn L. M. 2001. *House D of the Southeast Row House: Excavations at Fort Michilimackinac, 1989–1997*. Archaeological Completion Report Series No. 17. Mackinac State Historic Parks, Mackinac Island, MI.

———. 2003. *Keys to the Past: Archaeological Treasures of Mackinac*. Mackinac State Historic Parks, Mackinac Island, MI.

Farry, Andrew. 2005. "' . . . of difft. Bores & sorts': An Archaeological Study of Anglo-American Musket Balls." *New York History* 86(4):451–471.

———. 2005. "Regulars and 'Irregulars': British and Provincial Variability among Eighteenth-Century Military Frontiers." *Historical Archaeology* 39(2):16–32.

Faulkner, Alaric. 1981. "Pentagoet: A First Look at Seventeenth Century Acadian Maine." *Northeast Historical Archaeology* 10:51–57.

———. 1986. "Maintenance and Fabrication at Fort Pentagoet 1635–1654: Products of an Acadian Armorer's Workshop." *Historical Archaeology* 20(1):63–94.

Faulkner, Alaric, and Gretchen Faulkner. 1987. *The French at Pentagoet 1635–1674: An Archaeological Portrait of the Acadian Frontier*. Occasional Publications in Maine Archaeology 5. Augusta: Maine Historic Preservation Commission and the New Brunswick Museum.

Feister, Lois M. 1984a. "Building Material Indicative of Status Differentiation at the Crown Point Barracks." *Historical Archaeology* 18(1):103–107.

———. 1984b. "Material Culture of the British Soldier at 'His Majesty's Fort of Crown Point' on Lake Champlain, New York, 1759–1783." *Journal of Field Archaeology* 11(2):123–132.

Feister, Lois M., and Paul R. Huey. 1985. "Archaeological Testing at Fort Gage, a Provincial Redoubt of 1758 at Lake George, New York." *Bulletin and Journal of Archaeology for New York State* 90:40–59.

Fisher, Charles L. 1983. "Archaeology at New Windsor Cantonment: Construction and Social Reproduction at a Revolutionary War Encampment." *Northeast Historical Archaeology* 12:15–23.

———. 1984–85. "Archaeological Survey and Historic Preservation at the Site of a Revolutionary War Cantonment in New Windsor, New York." *North American Archaeologist* 6(1):25–39.

———. 1986a. *Material Objects, Ideology, and Everyday Life: Archaeology of the Continental Soldier at the New Windsor Cantonment*. Waterford, NY: New York State Office of Parks, Recreation and Historic Preservation, Bureau of Historic Sites, Peebles Island.

———. 1986b. "The Temple of Virtue: An Artifact of Social Conflict at the Last Cantonment of the Continental Army." *Man in the Northeast* 32:95–108.

———. 1987. "The Ceramics Collection from the Continental Army Cantonment at New Windsor, New York." *Historical Archaeology* 21(1):48–57.

———. 1995. "The Archaeology of Provincial Officers' Huts at Crown Point State Historic Site." *Northeast Historical Archaeology* 24:65–86.

———, ed. 2004. *"The Most Advantageous Situation in the Highlands": An Archaeological Study of Fort Montgomery State Historic Site*. Cultural Resources Survey Program Series No. 2, New York State Museum, Albany.

Foote, Shelby. 1974. *The Civil War: A Narrative*. New York: Random House.

Fox, Christopher D. 2000. "One Piece at a Time: The Restoration of the Archaeological Ceramics Collections of Fort Ticonderoga." *Bulletin of the Fort Ticonderoga Museum* 16(3):272–283.

Fox, Richard A., Jr. 1988. "History as Seen through Archeology: The Custer Battle." Ph.D. dissertation, Department of Archeology, University of Calgary, Calgary.

———. 1993. *Archaeology, History, and Custer's Last Battle*. Norman: University of Oklahoma Press.

Fox, Richard A., Jr., and Douglas D. Scott. 1991. "The Post-Civil War Battlefield Pattern: An Example from the Custer Battlefield." *Historical Archeology* 25(2):92–103.

Frurip, David J., Russell Malewicki, and Donald P. Heldman. 1983. *Colonial Nails from Michilimackinac: Differentiation by Chemical and Statistical Analysis*. Archaeological Completion Report Series No. 7. Mackinac Island State Park Commission, Mackinac Island, MI.

Fry, Bruce W. 1984. *"An Appearance of Strength": The Fortifications of Louisbourg*. 2 vols. Parks Canada Studies in Archaeology, Architecture and History. Ottawa: National Historic Parks and Sites Branch, Parks Canada.

Geier, Clarence R., Jr. 1994. "Toward a Social History of the Civil War: The Hatcher-Cheatham Site." In *Look to the Earth: Historical Archaeology and the American Civil*

War, ed. Clarence R. Geier Jr. and Susan B. Winter, pp. 191–214. Knoxville: University of Tennessee Press.

———. 2003. "Confederate Fortification and Troop Deployment in a Mountain Landscape: Fort Edward Johnson and Camp Shenandoah, April 1862." *Historical Archaeology* 37(3):31–45.

Geier, Clarence R., David G. Orr, and Matthew B. Reeves, eds. 2006. *Huts and History: The Historical Archaeology of Military Encampment During the American Civil War*. Gainesville: University Press of Florida.

Geier, Clarence R., and Stephen R. Potter, eds. 2000. *Archaeological Perspectives on the American Civil War*. Gainesville: University Press of Florida.

Geier, Clarence R., Jr., and Susan E. Winter, eds. 1994. *Look to the Earth: Historical Archaeology and the American Civil War*. Knoxville: University of Tennessee Press.

Gifford, Stanley M. 1955. *Fort Wm. Henry—A History*. Lake George, NY: Fort William Henry.

Gould, Richard A. 2007. *Disaster Archaeology*. Salt Lake City: University of Utah Press.

Gramly, Richard Michael. 1978. *Fort Laurens 1778-9: The Archaeological Record*. Richmond, VA: William Byrd Press.

Grange, Roger T., Jr. 1987. *Excavations at Fort Mackinac, 1980–1982: The Provision Storehouse*. Archaeological Completion Report Series No. 12. Mackinac Island State Park Commission, Mackinac Island, MI.

Greene, Jerome A., and Douglas D. Scott. 2004. *Finding Sand Creek*. Norman: University of Oklahoma Press.

Grimm, Jacob L. 1970. *Archaeological Investigations of Fort Ligonier, 1960–1965*. Annals of the Carnegie Museum 42. Pittsburgh, PA.

Griswold, William A. 2001. "The Archaeology of Military Politics: The Case of Castle Clinton." *Historical Archaeology* 35(4):105–117.

Halchin, Jill Y. 1985. *Excavations at Fort Michilimackinac, 1983–1985: House C of the Southeast Rowhouse, the Solomon-Levy-Parant House*. Archaeological Completion Report Series No. 11. Mackinac Island State Park Commission, Mackinac Island, MI.

Hamilton, T. M. 1976. *Firearms on the Frontier: Guns at Fort Michilimackinac 1715–1781*. Reports in Mackinac History and Archaeology No. 5. Mackinac Island State Park Commission, Mackinac Island, MI.

Hamilton, T. M., and K. O. Emery. 1988. *Eighteenth Century Gunflints from Fort Michilimackinac and Other Colonial Sites*. Archaeological Completion Report Series No. 13. Mackinac Island State Park Commission, Mackinac Island, MI.

Hanson, Lee H., Jr. 1972. "The Marquis de Vauban and Military Fortifications." *Northeast Historical Archaeology* 2(1):7–8.

Hanson, Lee H., Jr., and Dick Ping Hsu. 1975. *Casements and Cannonballs: Archeological Investigations at Fort Stanwix, Rome, New York*. Publications in Archeology 14. National Park Service, Washington, D.C.

Hargrave, Michael L., Lewis E. Somers, Thomas K. Larson, Richard Shields, and John Dendy. 2002. "The Role of Resistivity Survey in Historic Site Assessment and Management: An Example from Fort Riley, Kansas." *Historical Archaeology* 36(4):89–110.

Harral, Todd H. 1993. "Archaeological Evidence of Status Differentiation at American Revolutionary War Forts and Cantonments." Unpublished manuscript, Plymouth State University.

Harrington, Jean C. 1957. *New Light on Washington's Fort Necessity*. Richmond, VA: Eastern National Park and Monument Association.

———. 1962. *Search for the cittie of Ralegh* . . . National Park Service, Archeological Research Series 6.

———. 1976. "The Puzzle of Washington's Fort Necessity." *Archaeology* 29(3):178–185.

Harrington, Walter L. 1978. "Fort Dummer: An Archaeological Investigation of the First Permanent English Settlement in Vermont." In *New England Historical Archeology,* ed. by Peter Benes, pp. 86–94. Dublin Seminar for New England Folklife: Annual Proceedings, 1977. Boston: Boston University Scholarly Publications.

Hathaway, Allen. 2000. "Mutiny, Matthew Lyon, and a Missing Fort: Archaeological Identification Studies of Fort Jericho." *Journal of Vermont Archaeology* 3:52–60.

Hauser, Judith Ann. 1982. *Jesuit Rings from Fort Michilimackinac and Other European Contact Sites*. Archaeological Completion Report Series No. 5. Mackinac Island State Park Commission, Mackinac Island, MI.

Heldman, Donald P. 1977. *Excavations at Fort Michilimackinac, 1976: The Southeast and South Southeast Row Houses*. Archaeological Completion Report Series No. 1. Mackinac Island State Park Commission, Mackinac Island, MI.

———. 1978. *Excavations at Fort Michilimackinac, 1977: House One of the South Southeast Row House*. Archaeological Completion Report Series No. 2. Mackinac Island State Park Commission, Mackinac Island, MI.

———. 1980. "Coins at Michilimackinac." *Historical Archaeology* 14:82–107.

———. 1986. "Michigan's First Jewish Settlers: A View from the Solomon-Levy Trading House at Fort Michilimackinac, 1765–1781." *Journal of New World Archaeology* 6(4):21–33.

———. 1991. "The French in Michigan and Beyond: An Archaeological View from Fort Michilimackinac Toward the West." In *French Colonial Archaeology: The Illinois Country and the Western Great Lakes,* ed. John A. Walthall, pp. 201–217. Urbana: University of Illinois Press.

Heldman, Donald P., and Roger T. Grange, Jr. 1981. *Excavations at Fort Michilimackinac 1978–79: The Rue de la Babillarde*. Archaeological Completion Report Series No. 3. Mackinac Island State Park Commission, Mackinac Island, MI.

Heldman, Donald P., and William L. Minnerly. 1977. *The Powder Magazine at Fort Michilimackinac: Excavation Report*. Reports in Mackinac History and Archaeology No. 6. Mackinac Island State Park Commission, Mackinac Island, MI.

Herskovitz, Robert M. 1978. *Fort Bowie Material Culture*. Anthropological Papers of the University of Arizona 31. Tucson: University of Arizona Press.

Hicks, Brian, and Schuyler Kropf. 2002. *Raising the Hunley: The Remarkable History and Recovery of the Lost Confederate Submarine*. New York: Ballantine Books.

Hill, William H. 1929. *Old Fort Edward Before 1800*. Fort Edward, NY: Privately printed.

Howe, Dennis E. 1991. "The Archeology of a 1776 Cantonment of New Hampshire Regiments." *New Hampshire Archeologist* 32(1):1–25.

———. 1996. *This Ragged, Starved, Lousy, Pocky Army: The Archaeology of Soldiers' Huts and a Summary of Underwater Research at Mount Independence Historic Site.* Concord, NH: Printed Word.

Howe, Dennis E., Marjorie Robbins, and William C. Murphy. 1994. "The South Battery at Mount Independence." *Journal of Vermont Archaeology* 1:127–140.

Huey, Paul R. 1988. "Aspects of Continuity and Change in Colonial Dutch Material Culture at Fort Orange, 1624–1664." Ph.D. dissertation, Department of American Studies, University of Pennsylvania, Philadelphia.

———. 1991. "The Dutch at Fort Orange." In *Historical Archaeology in Global Perspective*, ed. Lisa Falk, pp. 21–67. Washington, DC: Smithsonian Institution Press.

———. 1998. "Fort Orange Archaeological Site National Historic Landmark." *Bulletin and Journal of Archaeology for New York State* 114:12–23.

Huntington, Tom. 2005. "The *Hunley*." *Invention & Technology* 20(4):38–46.

Jensen, Todd L. 2000. "Civil War Archaeology at Fort Pocahontas: Life between the Trenches." *Quarterly Bulletin of the Virginia Archaeological Society* 55:126–134.

Jordan, Robert Paul. 1986. "Ghosts on the Little Bighorn." *National Geographic* 170(6):786–813.

Judge, Joseph. 1988. "Exploring Our Forgotten Century." *National Geographic* 173(3):330–363.

Kaplan, Reid W., and Michael D. Coe. 1976. "Pictures of the Past: Artifact Density and Computer Graphics." *Historical Archaeology* 10:54–67.

Kelso, Gerald K. 1993. "Pollen Analysis in Historical Landscape Studies: Fort Necessity, Pennsylvania." *Park Science* 13(2):8–10.

Kelso, Gerald K., Audrey J. Horning, Andrew C. Edwards, Marley R. Brown III, and Martha W. McCarthy. 1998. "Exploratory Pollen Analysis of the Ditch of the 1665 Turf Fort, Jamestown, Virginia." *Northeast Historical Archaeology* 27:63–84.

Kelso, Gerald K., and Dick Ping Hsu. 1995. "Battlefield Palynology: Reinterpretation of British Earthworks, Saratoga National Historical Park, Stillwater, New York." *Northeast Historical Archaeology* 24:87–96.

Kelso, William M. 1993. *Jamestown Rediscovery Archaeological Project: The Search for the Site of James Fort (1607).* Jamestown, VA: Association for the Preservation of Virginia Antiquities.

———. 1995–2001. *Jamestown Rediscovery.* 7 vols. Jamestown, VA: Association for the Preservation of Virginia Antiquities.

———. 2006. *Jamestown: The Buried Truth.* Charlottesville: University of Virginia Press.

Kingsley, Ronald F. 1997. "An Archaeological Survey of the Land Approach to Mount Independence, 1776–1777." *Journal of Vermont Archaeology* 2:57–71.

———. 2000. "In Search of the Eighteenth Century Rowley Road, Shoreham Township, Addison County, Vermont." *Journal of Vermont Archaeology* 3:61–68.

Kingsley, Ronald F., and John P. Chiamulera. 2003. "An Investigation of the South Side Landing Area of Mount Independence, Orwell Township, Addison County, Vermont." *Journal of Vermont Archaeology* 4:19–40.

Kravic, Frank J. 1971. "Colonial Crown Point and Its Artifacts." *Northeast Historical Archaeology* 1(1):70–71.

Landon, David B. 1992. "Taphonomic Evidence for Site Formation Processes at Fort Christanna." *International Journal of Osteoarchaeology* 2:351–359.

Laumbach, Karl W. 2001. "Fire Fight at Hembrillo Basin." *Archaeology* 54(6):34–39.

Leach, Almon E. 2000. "Nail Identification at Old Fort Niagara." *Bulletin and Journal of Archaeology for New York State* 116:35–50.

Lees, William B., and Kathryn M. Kimery-Lees. 1992. "Regional Perspectives on the Fort Towson Sutler's Store and Residence, Frontier Site in Antebellum Eastern Oklahoma." *Plains Anthropologist* 29:13–24.

Lenik, Edward J. 1987. "An Admirable Police Maintained: Evidence of Sanitary Practices at the New Windsor Cantonment." *Northeast Historical Archaeology* 16:58–66.

Lesser, W. Hunter, Kim A. McBride, and Janet G. Brashler. 1994. "Cheat Summit Fort and Camp Allegheny: Early Civil War Encampments in West Virginia." In *Look to the Earth: Historical Archaeology and the American Civil War*, ed. Clarence R. Geier Jr. and Susan E. Winter, pp. 158–170. Knoxville: University of Tennessee Press.

Lewis, Clifford M. 1963. "Camp Allegheny: A Survey of a Confederate Winter Quarters." *West Virginia Archaeologist* 16:33–45.

Liston, Maria A., and Brenda J. Baker. 1995. "Reconstructing the Massacre at Fort William Henry, New York." *International Journal of Osteoarchaeology* 6:28–41.

Litt, Paul, Ronald F. Williamson, and Joseph W. A. Whitehorne. 1993. *Death at Snake Hill: Secrets from a War of 1812 Cemetery*. Toronto: Dundurn Press.

Lord, Philip, Jr. 1989. *War over Walloomscoick: Land Use and Settlement Pattern on the Bennington Battlefield—1777*. New York State Museum Bulletin 473. University of the State of New York, State Education Department, Albany.

Malakoff, David. 2009. "Investigating French and Indian War Forts." *American Archaeology* 13(1):33–38.

Malcarne, Don. 2003. "The British Attack at Essex, Connecticut & Related Archival/Archaeological Investigation." *Bulletin of the Archaeological Society of Connecticut* 65:31–40.

Manning-Sterling, Elise. 2004. "Fort Ticonderoga." *Council for Northeast Historical Archaeology Newsletter* 57:21–22. March.

Margolin, Samuel G. 1994. "Endangered Legacy: Virginia's Civil War Naval Heritage." In *Look to the Earth: Historical Archaeology and the American Civil War*, ed. Clarence R. Geier Jr. and Susan E. Winter, pp. 76–98. Knoxville: University of Tennessee Press.

Maxwell, Moreau S., and Lewis Binford. 1961. *Excavations at Fort Michilimackinac, Mackinac City, Michigan, 1959 Season*. Publications of the Museum, Michigan State University, Cultural Series Vol. 1, No. 1. East Lansing, MI.

McBride, Kim. 2006. "The Frontier Forts Project." *Council for Northeast Historical Archaeology Newsletter* 65: 17.

McBride, W. Stephen. 1994. "Civil War Material Culture and Camp Life in Central Kentucky: Archaeological Investigations at Camp Nelson." In *Look to the Earth: Historical Archaeology and the American Civil War*, ed. Clarence R. Geier Jr. and Susan E. Winter, pp. 130–157. Knoxville: University of Tennessee Press.

McBride, W. Stephen, and Kim A. McBride. 2006. "Civil War Housing Insights from Camp Nelson, Kentucky." In *Huts and History: The Historical Archaeology of Military*

Encampment During the American Civil War, ed. Clarence R. Geier, David G. Orr, and Matthew B. Reeves, pp. 136–171. Gainesville: University Press of Florida.

McCarthy, John P., Jeffrey B. Snyder, and Billy R. Roulette Jr. 1991. "Arms from Addison Plantation and the Maryland Militia on the Potomac Frontier." *Historical Archaeology* 25(1):66–79.

McLaughlin, Scott A. 2000. *History Told from the Depths of Lake Champlain: 1992–1993 Fort Ticonderoga–Mount Independence Submerged Cultural Resource Survey.* Ferrisburgh, VT: Lake Champlain Maritime Museum at Basin Harbor.

———. 2003. "Resume of a Seventeenth-Century Top-Secret Weapon: The Story of the Mount Independence Cannon." *Journal of Vermont Archaeology* 4:1–18.

McPherson, James M. 1988. *Battle Cry of Freedom: The Civil War Era.* New York: Oxford University Press.

Miller, Henry. 1991. "Tobacco Pipes from Popes Fort, St. Mary's City, Maryland: An English Civil War Site on the American Frontier." In *The Archaeology of the Clay Tobacco Pipe, XII: Chesapeake Bay.* British Archaeological Reports, Oxford.

Miller, J. Jefferson, II, and Lyle M. Stone. 1970. *Eighteenth-Century Ceramics from Fort Michilimackinac: A Study in Historical Archaeology.* Smithsonian Studies in History and Technology No. 4. Washington, DC.

Morand, Lynn L. 1994. *Craft Industries at Fort Michilimackinac, 1715–1781.* Archaeological Completion Report Series No. 15. Michigan State Historic Parks, Mackinac Island, MI.

Nash, Steve. 2004. "Battles Over Battlefields." *Archaeology* 57(5):24–29.

Nassaney, Michael S., William Cremin, Renee Kurtzweil, and Jose Antonio Brandao. 2003. "The Search for Fort St. Joseph (1691–1781) in Niles, Michigan." *Midcontinental Journal of Archaeology* 28(2):107–144.

Nassaney, Michael S., William M. Cremin, and Daniel P. Lynch. 2002–4. "The Identification of Colonial Fort St. Joseph, Michigan." *Journal of Field Archaeology* 29(3–4):309–321.

Nayler, Peter, comp. 1993. *Military Button Manufacturers from the London Directories, 1800–1899.* Archaeological Services, National Historic Sites. Ottawa: Canadian Heritage, Parks Canada.

Neely, Paula. 2008–9. "New Discovery Sheds Light on *Hunley's* Fate." *American Archaeology* 12(4):7.

Neumann, George C., and Frank J. Kravic. 1975. *Collector's Illustrated Encyclopedia of the American Revolution.* Texarkana, TX: Rebel Publishing.

Noël Hume, Ivor. 1994. *Martin's Hundred.* New York: Alfred A. Knopf.

Noël Hume, Ivor, and Audrey Noël Hume. 2001. *The Archaeology of Martin's Hundred.* 2 vols. Williamsburg, VA: Colonial Williamsburg Foundation.

O'Donnell, Michael J., and J. Duncan Campbell. 1996. *American Military Belt Plates.* Alexandria, VA: O'Donnell Publications.

Oeland, Glenn. 2002. "The *H. L. Hunley*: Secret Weapon of the Confederacy." *National Geographic* 202(1):82–101.

Orr, David G. 1994. "The Archaeology of Trauma: An Introduction to the Archaeology of the American Civil War." In *Look to the Earth: Historical Archaeology and the Ameri-*

can Civil War, ed. Clarence R. Geier Jr. and Susan B. Winter, pp. 21–36. Knoxville: University of Tennessee Press.

———. 2006. "Cabin in Command: The City Point Headquarters of Ulysses S. Grant." In *Huts and History: The Historical Archaeology of Military Encampment During the American Civil War,* ed. Clarence R. Geier, David G. Orr, and Matthew B. Reeves, pp. 244–261. Gainesville: University Press of Florida.

Parrington, Michael. 1979. "Geophysical and Aerial Prospecting Techniques at Valley Forge National Historical Park, Pennsylvania." *Journal of Field Archaeology* 6(2):193–201.

———. 1979–80. "Revolutionary War Archaeology at Valley Forge, Pennsylvania." *North American Archaeologist* 1(2):161–175.

Parrington, Michael, Helen Schenck, and Jacqueline Thibau. 1984. "The Material World of the Revolutionary War Soldier at Valley Forge." In *The Scope of Historical Archaeology,* ed. David G. Orr and Daniel G. Crozier, pp. 125–161. Philadelphia: Occasional Publication of the Department of Anthropology, Temple University.

Peña, Elizabeth S. 2006. "Wampum Diplomacy: The Historical and Archaeological Evidence for Wampum at Fort Niagara." *Northeast Historical Archaeology* 35:15–29.

Peiffer, Susan, and Ronald F. Williamson, eds. 1991. *Snake Hill: An Investigation of a Military Cemetery from the War of 1812.* Toronto: Dundurn Press.

Poirier, David A. 1976. Camp Reading: Logistics of a Revolutionary War Winter Encampment. *Northeast Historical Archaeology* 5(1–2):40–52.

Pollard, Tony, ed. 2009. *Culloden: The History and Archaeology of the Last Clan Battle.* Barnsley, UK: Pen & Sword Military.

Potter, Stephen R., and Douglas W. Owsley. 2000. "An Irishman Dies at Antietam: An Archaeology of the Individual." In *Archaeological Perspectives on the American Civil War*, ed. Clarence R. Geier Jr. and Stephen R. Potter, pp. 56–72. Gainesville: University Press of Florida.

Powell, Eric A. 2003. "Fortress on the Hudson." *Archaeology* 56(1):32–35.

Prentice, Guy, and Marie C. Prentice. 2000. "Far from the Battlefield: Archaeology at Andersonville Prison." In *Archaeological Perspectives on the American Civil War*, ed. Clarence R. Geier Jr. and Stephen R. Potter, pp. 166–187. Gainesville: University Press of Florida.

Raynor, Laura A., and Douglas J. Kennett. 2008. "Dietary Variability among a Sample of United States Soldiers during the War of 1812." *Historical Archaeology* 42(4):76–87.

Reeves, Matthew B. 2001. *Dropped and Fired: Archaeological Patterns of Militaria from Two Civil War Battles, Manassas National Battlefield Park, Manassas, Virginia.* Occasional Report, No. 15. Occasional Report Series of the Regional Archaeology Program, National Capital Region, National Park Service.

Rinehart, Charles J. 1990. *Crucifixes and Medallions: Their Role at Fort Michilimackinac.* Volumes in Historical Archaeology 11. Columbia: South Carolina Institute of Archaeology and Anthropology, University of South Carolina.

Rintels, David W. 1996. *Andersonville.* Baton Rouge: Gideon Books, in association with Louisiana State University Press.

Robinson, Willard B. 1977. *American Forts: Architectural Form and Function*. Urbana: University of Illinois Press.

Rogers Island Historical Association. 1986. *Exploring Rogers Island*. 2nd ed. Publication No. 2. Fort Edward, NY: Rogers Island Historical Association.

Romey, Kristin M. 2005. "The Dead of Snake Hill." *Archaeology* 58(3):42–49.

Rose, Mark. 2005. "The Forgotten Fight for America." *Archaeology* 58(1):46–51.

Rutsch, Edward S., and Kim M. Peters. 1977. "Forty Years of Archaeological Research at Morristown National Historical Park, Morristown, New Jersey." *Historical Archaeology* 11:15–38.

Rutsch, Edward S., and Sally Skinner. 1972. "Research Done in 1971 on Fort Nonsense." *Northeast Historical Archaeology* 2(1):35–43.

Scott, Douglas D. 1989. "An Officer's Latrine at Fort Larned and Inferences on Status." *Plains Anthropologist* 34:23–34.

———. 2003. "Oral Tradition and Archaeology: Conflict and Concordance Examples from Two Indian War Sites." *Historical Archaeology* 37(3):55–65.

Scott, Douglas D., and Richard A. Fox Jr. 1987. *Archaeological Insights into the Custer Battle: An Assessment of the 1984 Field Season*. Norman: University of Oklahoma Press.

Scott, Douglas D., Richard A. Fox Jr., Melissa A. Connor, and Dick Harmon. 1989. *Archaeological Perspectives on the Battle of The Little Bighorn*. Norman: University of Oklahoma Press.

Scott, Douglas D., P. Willey, and Melissa A. Connor. 1998. *They Died with Custer: Soldiers' Bones from the Battle of the Little Bighorn*. Norman: University of Oklahoma Press.

Scott, Elizabeth M. 1985. *French Subsistence at Fort Michilimackinac, 1715–1781: The Clergy and the Traders*. Archaeological Completion Report Series No. 9. Mackinac Island State Park Commission, Mackinac Island, MI.

———. 1991. "Such Diet as Befitted His Station as Clerk: The Archaeology of Subsistence and Cultural Diversity at Fort Michilimackinac, 1761–1781." Ph.D. dissertation, Department of Anthropology, University of Minnesota.

Scott, Patricia Kay. 1998. "Historic Contact Archaeological Deposits Within the Old Fort Niagara National Historic Landmark." *Bulletin and Journal of Archaeology for New York State* 114:45–57.

Scott, Stuart D., and Patricia Kay Scott. 1990. "A Fort Called Niagara." *Archaeology* 43(1):64–66, 84.

Scott, Stuart D., Patricia Kay Scott, James W. F. Smith, and James MacLeay. 1991. "Reorientation of Historical Maps of Old Fort Niagara Using Computer-Assisted Cartography." *Journal of Field Archaeology* 18(3):319–343.

Seidel, John L. 1983. "Archaeological Research at the 1778–79 Winter Cantonment of the Continental Artillery, Pluckemin, New Jersey." *Northeast Historical Archaeology* 12:7–14.

———. 1987. "The Archaeology of the American Revolution: A Reappraisal and Case Study at the Continental Artillery Cantonment of 1778–1779, Pluckemin, NJ." Ph.D. dissertation, Department of Anthropology, University of Pennsylvania.

Shugar, Aaron N., and Ariel O'Connor. 2008. "The Analysis of 18th-Century Glass Trade

Beads from Fort Niagara: Insight into Compositional Variation and Manufacturing Techniques." *Northeast Historical Archaeology* 37:58–68.

Sivilich, Daniel M. 1996. "Analyzing Musket Balls to Interpret a Revolutionary War Site." *Historical Archaeology* 30(2):101–109.

Sivilich, Daniel M., and Garry Wheeler Stone. n.d. *The Battle of Monmouth: The Archaeology of Molly Pitcher, the Royal Highlanders, and Colonel Cilley's Light Infantry.* Pamphlet. Freehold, NJ: BRAVO.

Smith, Gregory, and Lois Feister. 2004. "Introduction." In *"The Most Advantageous Situation in the Highlands": An Archaeological Study of Fort Montgomery State Historic Site,* ed. Charles L. Fisher, pp. 1–3. Cultural Resources Survey Program Series No. 2. New York State Museum, Albany.

Smith, Steven D. 2000. "The Submarine *H. L. Hunley.*" In *Archaeological Perspectives on the American Civil War,* ed. Clarence R. Geier and Stephen R. Potter, pp. 29–42. Gainesville: University Press of Florida.

Smith, Steven D., Christopher Ohm Clement, and Stephen R. Wise. 2003. "GPS, GIS and the Civil War Battlefield Landscape: A South Carolina Low Country Example." *Historical Archaeology* 37(3):14–30.

Snow, Dean R. 1977. *Archaeological Atlas of the Saratoga Battlefield.* Department of Anthropology, State University of New York at Albany.

———. 1981. "Battlefield Archeology." *Early Man* 3(1):18–21.

South, Stanley. 1979. "The Search for Sixteenth Century Santa Elena." *Conference on Historic Site Archaeology Papers 1978* 13:25–37.

Starbuck, David R. 1988. "The American Headquarters for the Battle of Saratoga." *Northeast Historical Archaeology* 17:16–39.

———. 1989. *The Ferris Site on Arnold's Bay.* Basin Harbor, VT: Lake Champlain Maritime Museum.

———. 1990a. "The General Hospital at Mount Independence: 18th Century Health Care at a Revolutionary War Cantonment." *Northeast Historical Archaeology* 19:50–68.

———. 1990b. "A Retrospective on Archaeology at Fort William Henry, 1952–1993: Retelling the Tale of *The Last of the Mohicans.*" *Northeast Historical Archaeology* 20:8–26.

———. 1993a. "Building Independence on Lake Champlain." *Archaeology* 46(5):60–63.

———. 1993b. "Anatomy of a Massacre." *Archaeology* 46(6):42–46.

———. 1994a. "The Identification of Gender at Northern Military Sites of the Late 18th Century." In *Those of Little Note: Gender, Race, and Class in Historical Archaeology,* ed. Elizabeth Scott, pp. 115–128. Tucson: University of Arizona Press.

———. 1994b. "The Rogers Island Archaeological Site: Transforming Myths into Strategies for Interpreting and Managing a Major Encampment from the French and Indian War." In *Cultural Resource Management,* ed. Jordan E. Kerber, pp. 243–260. Westport, CT: Bergin & Garvey.

———, ed. 1995. *Archeology in Fort Edward.* Queensbury, NY: Adirondack Community College.

———. 1996. "Four Years of Archaeological Research on Rogers Island, an Encampment of the French and Indian War." In *A Northeastern Millennium: History and Archaeology for Robert E. Funk,* ed. Christopher Lindner and Edward V. Curtin. *Journal of Middle Atlantic Archaeology* 12:149–161.

————. 1997a. "America's Forgotten War." *Archaeology* 50(1):60–63.

————. 1997b. "Military Hospitals on the Frontier of Colonial America." *Expedition* 39(1):33–45.

————. 1998. "The Big Dig: Looking for Traces of Fort William Henry's Brutal Past." *Adirondack Life* 29(6):44–49, 77–78.

————. 1999a. "Early Military Sites Archaeology in New York State: An Interview with Richard J. Koke." *Northeast Historical Archaeology* 28:71–88.

————. 1999b. *The Great Warpath: British Military Sites from Albany to Crown Point.* Hanover, NH: University Press of New England.

————. 1999c. "Military Archaeology of America's Colonial Wars." In *Old and New Worlds*, ed. Geoff Egan and R. L. Michael, pp. 195–202. Oxford: Oxbow Books.

————. 2001. "Beneath the Bubblegum." *Archaeology* 54(1):22–23.

————. 2002a. "Hallowed Ground: Exploring Lake George Battlefield Park." *Adirondack Life: 2002 Annual Guide to the Great Outdoors* 33(4):14–16, 18–20, 22.

————. 2002b. *Massacre at Fort William Henry.* Hanover, NH: University Press of New England.

————. 2004a. *Rangers and Redcoats on the Hudson.* Hanover, NH: University Press of New England.

————. 2004b. "The Scientific Investigation of Jane McCrea." *Journal of the Washington County Historical Society*, pp. 4–23. Fort Edward, NY.

————. 2005. "The Archaeology of America's Colonial Wars." In *Unlocking the Past: Celebrating Historical Archaeology in North America*, ed. Lu Ann De Cunzo and John Jameson Jr., pp. 151–159. Gainesville: University Press of Florida.

————. 2006. "Fort Edward Martyr Mystery." *Adirondack Life* 37(8):48–52.

————. 2007. "Commerce of War: Inside a Colonial Merchant's House." *Archaeology* 60(4):41–43.

————. 2008a. "Colonial America at War! 'Sutlers' Provided Fort Edward Soldiers with Much-Needed Relief." *Annual Journal of the Washington County Historical Society*, pp. 4–11. Fort Edward, NY.

————. 2008b. "The 'Massacre' at Fort William Henry—History, Archaeology, and Reenactment." *Expedition* 50(1):17–25.

————. 2010. *Excavating the Sutlers' House: Artifacts of the British Armies in Fort Edward and Lake George.* Hanover, NH: University Press of New England.

Starbuck, David R., and William C. Murphy. 1994. "Archaeology at Mount Independence: An Introduction." *Journal of Vermont Archaeology* 1:115–126.

Steegmann, A. Theodore, Jr., and P. A. Haseley. 1988. "Stature Variation in the British American Colonies: French and Indian War Records, 1755–1763." *American Journal of Physical Anthropology* 75:413–421.

Steele, Ian K. 1990. *Betrayals: Fort William Henry and the "Massacre."* New York: Oxford University Press.

Sterling, Bruce B., and Bernard W. Slaughter. 2000. "Surveying the Civil War: Methodological Approaches at Antietam Battlefield." In *Archaeological Perspectives on the American Civil War*, ed. Clarence R. Geier Jr. and Stephen R. Potter, pp. 305–322. Gainesville: University Press of Florida.

Stone, Lyle M. 1974. *Fort Michilimackinac 1715–1781: An Archaeological Perspective on the Revolutionary Frontier*. Anthropological Series, Vol. 2. Michigan State University, East Lansing, in cooperation with Mackinac Island State Park Commission, Mackinac Island, MI.

Sullivan, Catherine. 1986. *Legacy of the Machault: A Collection of 18th-Century Artifacts*. Parks Canada Studies in Archaeology, Architecture and History. Ottawa: National Historic Parks and Sites Branch, Parks Canada.

Synenki, Alan T., and Sheila Charles. 1983. *Archeological Collections Management at Morristown National Historical Park New Jersey*. ACMP Series No. 2. Boston: Division of Cultural Resources, North Atlantic Regional Office, National Park Service, U.S. Department of the Interior.

Thacher, James, M.D. 1862. *Military Journal of the American Revolution to Which Has Been Added the Life of Washington*. Hartford, CT: Hurlbut, Williams.

Todish, Timothy J. 2002. *The Annotated and Illustrated Journals of Major Robert Rogers*. Fleischmanns, NY: Purple Mountain Press.

Troiani, Don. 2001. *Military Buttons of the American Revolution*. Gettysburg, PA: Thomas Publications.

Utley, Robert M. 1994. *Little Bighorn Battlefield: A History and Guide to the Battle of the Little Bighorn*. Little Bighorn Battlefield National Monument, Montana. Produced by the Division of Publications, National Park Service. Washington, D.C: U.S. Department of the Interior.

Vauban, Sebastien de Prestre de. 1968. *Manual of Siegecraft and Fortification*. Ann Arbor: University of Michigan Press.

Wells, Peter S. 2003. *The Battle that Stopped Rome*. New York: W. W. W. Norton.

Whitaker, John M. F. 1998. *The Functions of Four Colonial Yards of the Southeast Row House, Fort Michilimackinac, Michigan*. Archaeological Completion Report Series No. 16. Mackinac State Historic Parks, Mackinac Island, MI.

Whittaker, William E. 2009. "Testing the Effectiveness of Ground-Penetrating Radar at Three Dragoon Forts in Iowa and Wisconsin." *Historical Archaeology* 43(4):56–74.

Willey, P., and Douglas D. Scott. 1996. "'The Bullets Buzzed Like Bees': Gunshot Wounds in Skeletons from the Battle of the Little Bighorn." *International Journal of Osteoarchaeology* 6(1):15–27.

Williams, J. Mark, and Gary Shapiro. 1982. *A Search for the Eighteenth Century Village at Michilimackinac: A Soil Resistivity Survey*. Archaeological Completion Report Series, No. 4. Mackinac Island State Park Commission, Mackinac Island, MI.

Winter, Susan E. 1994. "Civil War Fortifications and Campgrounds on Maryland Heights, the Citadel of Harpers Ferry." In *Look to the Earth: Historical Archaeology and the American Civil War*, ed. Clarence R. Geier Jr. and Susan E. Winter, pp. 101–129. Knoxville: University of Tennessee Press.

Wolkomir, Richard. 1998. "In Vermont, a Valiant Stand for Freedom." *Smithsonian* 29(4):54–64.

Zaboly, Gary Stephen. 2004. *A True Ranger: The Life and Many Wars of Major Robert Rogers*. Garden City Park, NY: Royal Blockhouse.

Index

DAVID R. STARBUCK, associate professor of anthropology and sociology at Plymouth State University in New Hampshire, is the author of eight books, including *Massacre at Fort William Henry, Rangers and Redcoats on the Hudson,* and *Excavating the Sutlers' House.*

THE AMERICAN EXPERIENCE IN ARCHAEOLOGICAL PERSPECTIVE
Edited by Michael S. Nassaney

The books in this series explore an event, process, setting, or institution that was significant in the formative experience of contemporary America. Each volume will frame the topic beyond an individual site and attempt to give the reader a flavor of the theoretical, methodological, and substantive issues that researchers face in their examination of that topic or theme. These books will be comprehensive overviews that will allow serious students and scholars to get a good sense of contemporary and past inquiries on a broad theme in American history and culture.

The Archaeology of Collective Action, by Dean J. Saitta (2007)
The Archaeology of Institutional Confinement, by Eleanor Conlin Casella (2007)
The Archaeology of Race and Racialization in Historic America, by Charles E. Orser Jr. (2007)
The Archaeology of North American Farmsteads, by Mark D. Groover (2008)
The Archaeology of Alcohol and Drinking, by Frederick H. Smith (2008)
The Archaeology of American Labor and Working-Class Life, by Paul A. Shackel (2009; first paperback edition, 2011)
The Archaeology of Clothing and Bodily Adornment in Colonial America, by Diana DiPaolo Loren (2010; first paperback edition, 2011)
The Archaeology of American Capitalism, by Christopher N. Matthews (2010)
The Archaeology of Forts and Battlefields, by David R. Starbuck (2011; first paperback edition, 2012)
The Archaeology of Consumer Culture, by Paul R. Mullins (2011)
The Archaeology of Antislavery Resistance, by Terrance M. Weik (2012)

www.ingramcontent.com/pod-product-compliance
Lightning Source LLC
Chambersburg PA
CBHW021405090426
42742CB00009B/1013